Stories, Quips, and Quotes to Lift the Heart

hum♥R

for a m♥m's heart

Stories, Quips, and Quotes to Lift the Heart

hum♥R

for a m♥m's heart

Compiled by Shari McDonald

Illustrated by Kristen Myers

HOWARD
PUBLISHING CO.

Our purpose at Howard Publishing is to:

- *Increase faith* in the hearts of growing Christians
- *Inspire holiness* in the lives of believers
- *Instill hope* in the hearts of struggling people everywhere

Because He's coming again!

Humor for a Mom's Heart © 2002 by Howard Publishing Co., Inc.
All rights reserved. Printed in the United States of America

Published by Howard Publishing Co., Inc.,
3117 North 7th Street, West Monroe, Louisiana 71291-2227

06 07 08 09 10 11   10

Library of Congress Cataloging-in-Publication Data

Hum[o]r for a m[o]m's heart : stories, quips, and quotes to lift the heart / various authors.
    p. cm.
  On t.p. "hum[o]r" and m[o]m's appear with a heart in place of the letter "o".
  ISBN 1-58229-266-3
  1. American wit and humor.

PN6165 .H85 2002
818'.602083520431--dc21

2002027551

Compiled by Shari MacDonald
Cover art by Kristen Myers
Illustrated by Kristen Myers
Interior design by LinDee Loveland and John Luke

Unless otherwise noted, Scripture quotations are taken from the Holy Bible, New International Version. Copyright © 1973, 1978, 1984 International Bible Society. Used by permission of Zondervan Bible Publishers. Scriptures marked KJV are taken from The Holy Bible, Authorized King James Version, © 1961 by The National Publishing Co.

Contents

Chapter 4: Of Moms and Words

Chapter 5: Furry Fun

Chapter 6: Caution: Mother on the Loose

Chapter 7: The Joys of Parenthood

Chapter 8: Mothering Rule #29: Embarrass Your Kids

Contents

Chapter 9: Mothering Rule #30: Get Embarrassed by Your Kids

Chapter 10: Life with Mr. Comedy (a.k.a. "Dad")

Chapter 11: Cooking Up Comedy

Chapter 12: Family Frivolity

Chapter 13: Those Amusing Adolescents

Chapter 14: Kids Will Be Kids

Chapter 15: Where There's Motherhood

Chapter 16: St. Mom

Chapter 17: Holy Motherhood

Chapter 18: Smiling Strength

Contributors—235

Source Notes—239

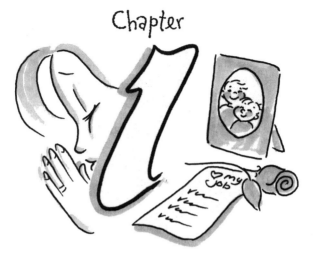

The Toughest Job You'll Ever Adore

The quickest way for a mother to get her children's attention is to sit down and look comfortable.

—LANE OLINGHOUSE

I Am Mommy, Hear Me Roar

Nancy Kennedy

A long time ago, I gave up using the name on my birth certificate and just started referring to myself as Mommy. As in:

"Come give Mommy a kiss."

"Tell Mommy where it hurts."

"I told you Mommy's ears can't hear whining."

"Mommy's face looks like this because Mommy just found out that somebody used her lace tablecloth to wipe off fingernail polish."

I knew I wasn't alone on that either. I know for a fact that none of my friends have names. We greet each other in the market:

"Hi, Sarah's mom!"

"Hi, Laura's mom!"

The vet even calls me "Blackie's mom."

I may not have a real name, but you know who I am. There's a container of Gak dumped in a corner of my living room carpet and the moldy remains of a peach deemed too gross to eat stuffed in the cushions of my couch. I walk around the house with dryer lint and used Q-tips in the pocket of my robe. I spend the majority of my day behind the wheel of a car—traveling hundreds of miles to and from softball practice, cheerleading practice, and trips to the market—yet never leave the city limits. I can't do a quadratic equation, but I can tell you how to get to Sesame Street.

My prayers are often frantic and generally specific. ("Lord, please help my child throw up in the bucket and not on the wall.") At times I pray to be made invisible, like during PTA

I know you know me. I wash my children's faces with spit and my thumb.

meetings when they need someone to chair the fifth grade fundraising car wash or during the Christmas program when it's my child up on stage singing, "Let there be peace on earth and let it begin with me," as she proceeds to slug the boy standing next to her.

I know you know me. I wash my children's faces with spit and my thumb. Pick at the dirt behind their ears. Whine about their whining. Nag about their nagging. Worry that I'll never live to see the day they'll change their underwear without coercion or threats of bodily harm.

I have eyes in the back of my head and a nose that can sniff out doggy doo-doo on a sneakered foot fifty yards away. I have ears that can hear Oreo cookies being eaten underneath the cov-

ers by a child who is supposedly asleep. With just one sideways glance, I can tell who sharpened her crayon with my eyeliner pencil sharpener and who accidentally-on-purpose let the bathroom sink overflow.

A few years ago, you would have recognized me as the one with strained chicken and peas plastered in my hair and a faraway look in my eyes, as I dreamed of a life that was not planned around nap time and late night feedings. I was the one who, when asked by a poll-taker to name my favorite male television performer, answered without hesitation, "Ernie from *Sesame Street.*"

Once upon a time I had a stomach that didn't fall to the floor. Once, I had hips that didn't serve as a baby saddle and a shelf for grocery bags. Once, I could even take a bath. Alone. All by myself. Without someone pounding on the closed door, asking if she could use the blue food coloring or "just wondering" if Super Glue ruins dining room tables.

If you looked in my closet you'd find baggy sweats with elastic waists; big, long sweaters; and pull-on pants. Forget Bill Blass and Anne Klein, give me Hanes Her Way any day.

You know who I am. I eat standing up. "Breakfast" consists of the soggy cereal left in bowls on the kitchen table, the ends of bread left in the bag, and blobs of strawberry jam scraped from the counter. I grab lunch on the run from a drive-through window and nibble on dinner as I cook it. I finish everyone else's ice cream, then wonder why I can't ever seem to lose weight.

Don't tell anyone, but I live for bedtime. I yearn for the sounds of a child's slumber. I long for my own head to hit the pillow. I pine for (yawn)…zzzzz.

You know me. I'm the one with the knot in her stomach,

praying her child will figure out how to turn over on the playground turnover bar so she won't be humiliated in front of her classmates during gym class. I'm the one who drinks the powdered milk so the rest of the family can have the "real" stuff. I'm the one who eagerly counted the days until both daughters went to school, then cried when that day finally arrived.

I'm the one who willingly suffered through morning sickness, swollen ankles, uncontrollable crying jags, and overwhelming desires for lemon meringue pie and out-of-season blackberries. (Not to mention pushing a bowling ball through a part of my body a bowling ball doesn't normally fit—twice.)

I'm the one frightened voices call for in the middle of the night. I'm the one who changes wet sheets at three in the morning, rocks a nightmare-stricken preschooler back to sleep at four, then gets up at five to let the dog out.

I'm the one who, despite an utterly selfish nature and a propensity toward evil (in addition to an inadequacy in and of myself and a definite lack of experience), God chose as caretaker, teacher, and nurturer for two totally dependent little sinners.

> I'm the one who, despite an utterly selfish nature, God chose as nurturer for two totally dependent little sinners.

With apologies to the Peace Corps, I have the toughest job anyone will ever love. I am battle-weary from refereeing squabbles over who did or did not do the dishes last and battle-scarred from getting smacked in the thigh by a line-driven softball during backyard batting practice. Still, I endure.

Who am I? I am a cooker of oatmeal and cleaner of soap scum. A taxi driver, spider killer, purchaser of folders with pockets and prongs, pencil finder, and dental appointment maker.

Loudest cheerleader and most fervent pray-er, encourager of dreams and holder of hands. I am a tear wiper and boo-boo kisser, the toothbrushing gestapo and an example of faith. You know who I am.

I am a mother.

Motherhood's Unsolved Mysteries

Karen Scalf Linamen

Before I was a parent, I had no children, but I had lots of theories about parenting.

Now I have two children and no theories.

Actually, the person in my home who believes she knows the most about parenting is my fourteen-year-old daughter. Of course, she thinks she knows the most about everything under the sun. She will, no doubt, get smarter and smarter until the day she gives birth to her first child. At that point, it is virtually guaranteed that she will experience a massive knowledge deficit.

Some experts believe that this "brain drain" is, in some mysterious fashion, related to the detachment of the placenta during childbirth. Others believe it is actually triggered in the months and years following childbirth, probably as a result of a prolonged exposure to seven-foot birds and purple herbivores.

Whatever the reason, the bottom line is this:

Even though you and I grew up believing that Father (and Mother) really did know best, once we became parents ourselves we suddenly discovered the Big Secret: Moms and dads don't have a clue. We just make that stuff up about being omniscient to keep knowledgeable kids in check until they, too, become parents and experience a two-thirds drop in their IQ. Then they can be in charge.

The truth is, I've been a parent long enough to know that every morning brings with it some new challenge for which I am nominally prepared. Why can't kids come with instructions? Both of my babies came home from the hospital with one of those nasal suction devices they tried to adopt as pacifiers. Why don't doctors send babies home with something their parents can really use…like a how-to manual?

I am constantly amazed by the number of times my kids have left me scratching my head in confusion or wonder (and I'm not even referring to the time they put dish detergent in the shampoo bottle. That's another head-scratching story altogether).

Do I know best? Sometimes I think I don't know squat.

A few of the many topics about which I don't have a clue include the following:

How serious is it when a two-year-old has a toe fetish? When Kacie was two, several times a day she demanded to have her shoes and socks removed so she could examine her feet. Is she destined to spend her adult life wearing sandals for easy access? When she's in seventh grade and has to write an essay on "Someone I Admire," will she choose Imelda Marcos? And is podiatry a good career choice for someone with a foot fetish, or does that border on the unethical?

And that's not the only mystery.

What in the world does it mean when you are setting the table for company and find a hard glob of chewed gum under the rim of your best china? Whose gum is it? Your teenage son's? When did he last eat on the good china anyway? And if it wasn't him, could one of your previous guests have done it? Shouldn't the dishwasher have melted the gum and whisked it away when the plate was washed? And if chewed gum is indeed impervious to scalding soapy water, then how long has it been there? Was it there when you served your Christmas dinner to your in-laws or when you entertained your husband's boss last month?

Where do all the missing socks go?

Why is meat loaf served at a friend's house more enticing to your kids than pizza served at home?

What do teenage girls do in the bathroom for three hours?

And what exactly does it mean when your ten-year-old loses a tooth at school, brings it home in a tiny plastic box, and then leaves it sitting for two months in a corner of your kitchen counter? When Kaitlyn was ten, my countertop was adorned with an abandoned baby molar for two months. I had to ask myself, did Kaitlyn forget it was there? Had she lost sleep at night wondering where she left her tooth and longing for her dollar from the tooth fairy? If so, why hadn't she mentioned it to me? What if she didn't think her tooth was lost? What if she knew exactly where it was? What if a visit from the tooth fairy was the last thing on her mind? What if…what if my baby's growing up?

From potty training dilemmas to disciplinary decisions to debates about dating, driving, and the decorative piercing of body parts, motherhood offers a smorgasbord of challenging questions that promise to stump even the wisest of moms and dads.

Maybe Robert Young had all the answers when he was raising Princess, Kitten, and Bud.

But for the rest of us, parenting is a leap of faith…an unending series of mysteries…an adventure that takes us daily to our wits' end and beyond.

Do fathers know best? Do mothers?

No way.

But there is one Father who does.

It's an amazing thing, but when we enter into a relationship with God's own Son, Jesus, we find ourselves adopted into the family of God. What we used to think of as some nebulous cosmic power suddenly becomes real to us in a way we never could have imagined. The Force becomes family. That higher power turns out to be a heavenly Father. We discover that the distant deity is more along the lines of…well, actually, a dad.

I may be a mom, but I don't come close to having all the answers I need in my life. I need a heavenly Father to help me make sense of it all…to help me meet the challenge of raising my family…to help me achieve my potential as a parent, spouse, and human being.

You need that kind of a Dad, too.

He's got all the answers, after all. And whatever answers he doesn't give us here on earth, I'm sure he'll be willing to provide once we get to heaven.

Just remind me, when we get there, in case it's a long time from now and I forget to ask.

I'd still love to know about that gum under my china.

The Husband's Progress

Chris Fabry

As I drove through the expressways of this world, hurrying on my way to work, I lighted on a certain rest area, where I parked and drifted off to sleep. As I slept, I dreamed a dream.

I dreamed, and behold, I beheld myself changed, with long hair, a shapely figure, and a feeling that I was on duty twenty-four hours a day. I beheld myself (but it was actually my wife), and boy, was I tired.

It was still dark, and I was cradling our infant son, who was coughing and making all kinds of rude noises in the night. Another body stirred beside me, but I said, "It's okay; go back to sleep. I'll take care of the baby." And I did care for him, there in the darkness with no one to thank me, no one to remember my sacrifice.

I comforted the child with persistent "Shhs" and a loving pat no one saw, for no one was awake except me and the screaming

child, and behold, he did stink. It was in the stillness of the night, with the coughing and the sputtering, and a quick snap of adhesive on a new diaper, that I felt my lips move in prayer for this little one and for each precious life under my care. And then I sang, sweetly, gently, and the child in my arms rolled his eyes back and gave up the fight. He lay there on my chest until I stood to lay him down. But he woke up again, and I was up the rest of the night with this sleeping lump on top of me. Strangely enough, I didn't mind.

As the sun rose, I looked, and behold, I saw all the duties for the day listed under the refrigerator magnet. I saw other things not listed that no one would do if I didn't, such as diaper changes too numerous to mention, laundry to be picked up, sorted, washed, dried, sorted, folded, and placed again in respective chambers. I saw dirty dishes, empty lunch pails, report cards to sign, and notes to teachers waiting to be stuffed in backpacks. I saw coats and hats and scarves and gloves flying from a box near the doorway as my children scrambled out the door.

In the midst of these duties, I saw tenderness. My child made a mess on the kitchen table of brown sugar, microwaved marshmallows, and cat food. (Don't ask about this one, I'm still trying to figure it out.) I took her by the hand, and instead of scolding her, I cleaned her up and brought out Play-Doh. Then I took a moment to stand in the corner and watch her play. After lunch I bent down on that floor and picked up all the Play-Doh, that is, all the Play-Doh that was not ground into the tile. I found a few peas and Cheerios, too. Instead of complaining, I thought about the day when I would long for the chore of scraping Play-Doh and chasing dried peas across the kitchen floor and into the heating vent. I brushed back a tear.

As I looked at this scene, I was thinking all the while that this was not the way I would do it. But there I was, doing all these things in my dream, with my shapely figure, and still feeling like I was on duty twenty-four hours a day. (I cannot stress this enough.)

When the wee ones were napping, I didn't fritter away my time in any way. There were books and magazines to read, and TV soaps to watch, but I spent a few minutes reading the Bible and then went to work at the small business I had begun for the purpose of bringing in some extra income for the family. I returned phone calls and faxes, and opened the mail. There were bills to pay, invoices to write, and paperwork to file.

Soon, my older children came home, and I felt like a coat tree as they clung to me like koalas. They each told me things about their day that I have never heard before, because you just don't tell those types of things to fathers. But they were telling me, and the experience was a blessed revelation.

While I busied myself about the kitchen, getting snacks, cleaning spills, and answering homework questions, my husband arrived. He had sort of a kingly presence about him, as if we were all supposed to fall down at his feet and bring an offering. But I kissed him sweetly and welcomed him home and talked about his day as if all the things I had done were of no importance.

Oh, you should have heard the things he thought were important! The children were growing up before his eyes, and he didn't even notice it; but I bit my tongue and prayed he would soon discover this fact.

I felt tired, but there was no respite. I took the baby to the doctor and dragged the rest of the troops along so my husband could "get a little work done." When I came back from the pharmacy with an armload of medicine and the whining masses, he

sat on the couch, still in his work clothes, reading the paper. The shelf I had asked him to put up three months ago stood in the corner of the closet. This is the same closet that has no door because the screws are stripped and the door now stands in the laundry room.

The vacuum cleaner also stood like a lonely soldier by the couch, and I wondered why he hadn't fixed the little rattle that now sounds like a Howitzer every time we turn the thing on.

I realized he didn't understand when he spoke to me in a not-so-pleasant voice.

"Where did you go?" he asked. "You had three calls."

I thought I would have a coronary right then and there, and probably would have if I weren't in this other person's shoes. But I quietly explained and then organized the medicine so any animal with a brain the size of a chestnut would be able to dole out the correct dosages. Then I prepared dinner and put it on the table.

After dinner I gave the baby a bath and once again picked up clothes, toys, shoes, and books. I asked my husband to dispense the different medication while I prepared the vaporizers for each room. I

> I organized the medicine so any animal with a brain would be able to dole out the correct dosages.

felt a bit angry the third time he asked how much each child should get, but again, I bit my tongue and gave him detailed information.

When, at last, I laid my weary body in the bed, after brushing and flossing, of course, I felt something strange on my shoulder and was startled to find my husband's hand there and him saying in a rather breathless voice, "Hello." This was the voice of passion.

Behold, I yelped, for I could not understand how one person could plumb such depths of insensitivity. My yelp then woke the sickest child, who again slumbered on my chest through the night while my husband snored and my children breathed the vaporized air. What surprised me most was the depth to which I would serve, with little thanks and no pay.

I heard a honking sound, and immediately I awoke from my dream at the rest area. I saw that I was late for a meeting, and I rushed to be on time. Before I went into the conference room, I stopped by a phone and dialed the familiar number.

The ringing ceased, and I heard the congested cry of a small child, and a pleasant voice said, "Hello?"

"Hi, it's me," I said, emotion welling up within me.

"Oh, hi!" she said, and my heart felt like I had just hit a triple to right field. I wanted to tell her about my dream and all the things I had learned—the ways I had been insensitive to her, the demanding things I had no reason or right to demand. The way I had let her down and failed to pick up my share of the work at home.

"I just wanted to say…," I said, faltering.

"You wanted to say what?"

"Well…uh…I wanted to call before I went into this meeting and say…"

"Yes?"

"I-I wanted to ask what we're having for dinner tonight."

She paused for a moment, and a little piece of me died holding that phone. There was a tiny bit of pain in her voice that I would never have noticed had I not dreamt about her life.

"Chicken," she finally said. "I think chicken and rice, with that seasoning the children like."

"That sounds great," I said. "I'll try to be home early."

"Oh?"

"Yeah. Maybe I can feed the kids dinner and let you go out with one of your friends. Would you like that?"

She didn't say anything. I thought she might need a defibrillator, but in a moment she caught her breath and managed to choke out, "That would be great, honey. That would be so great."

I hung up the phone and headed into the meeting. As I sat down and put my notes in order, I straightened my tie and noticed a small red stain on the pocket of my shirt. It looked very much like cherry-flavored children's aspirin, and I paused there in the conference room at the office and prayed. I asked God to never again let me take my wife for granted. I asked him to give me the strength to give her that night off. And I prayed that I would never again assume that it's her duty to get the kids dressed for church on Sunday.

Home Is Where the Humor Is

Everyone can keep house better than her mother, till she trieth.

—THOMAS FULLER

Why Coupons Are Ruining My Life

Charlene Ann Baumbich

I have this cabinet above my stove that I cannot see into without jumping up into the air. I can reach the bottles stored in front if I stand on my tippy toes, but I cannot see what's behind them. Hence, that cabinet is used to store things I don't use very often. Things such as Tabasco sauce, Worcestershire sauce, steak sauce, soy sauce, red hot sauce, vinegar (apple and white), olive oil, pure sesame oil, cooking sherry, Elmer's glue—and coupons.

Consider this: Relationships (even some blood relationships) have been strained because of those lousy coupons. For instance, I can hardly stand to visit my favorite cousin anymore, her and her shoe boxes and file folders neatly organizing volumes of alphabetized coupons. I tell you, her dedication to those cut out, rip off, get-'em-in-the-mail little pieces of paper riddles me with guilt.

And so, no more can I just sit back and relax. I feel obligated to tackle every magazine and evening newspaper with not only my glasses, but a pair of scissors for those nasty "fifteen cents off" bulletins that rear their ugly heads every other paragraph.

George and my diets have been seriously deregulated by boxes and bags of things I would never have plucked off the grocers' shelves without the incentive of those devilish enticers.

Should my family ever want to eat out, heaven forbid we should pick a place for which we don't have a coupon. Even if our taste buds are hankering for a nice steak dinner we have often had to swallow down pizza or chicken in response to "large for a medium price" or a "value bucket coupon."

A simple trip to the grocery store can end up in a guilt-ridden sleepless night because I have: 1) left the coupons on the kitchen table; 2) forgotten to hand them to the checkout person; 3) had the checker discover most of them had expired in 1972; or 4) shopped myself into exhaustion at a number of stores because I was determined to have items 1, 2, or 3 but could not find the product.

> A simple trip to the grocery store can end up in a guilt-ridden sleepless night.

Our budget, which should be enhanced by coupons, has been dented by coupon accessories. I have purchased three coupon organizers because I always think each will inspire me to organize, which it does not. I also am the proud owner of four nifty coupon clippers that I can't ever find, which is why I own four of them.

Coupons are ruining my life. And if their clutter and guilt-producing powers alone aren't threatening enough, now they've

almost killed me—literally. You see, the coupons (and they probably number in the hundreds by now) are up in this cabinet so I don't have to look at them and be exposed to their power. I add to them religiously. I use them, if I am to be honest, almost never.

On a recent dark and stormy afternoon when I was alone in the house and preparing a shopping list, I heard an eery voice say, "You're not seriously going to buy instant coffee without taking one of our more than twenty coupons for coffee, are you?" And so, I approached "the cabinet."

Stretching my body to its maximum height, I pushed aside the Worcestershire sauce with my fingertips. A few coupons fluttered to my feet. They were not the coffee coupons; but they were coupons that reminded me that I wanted to try "Golden Goopers with a Tad More Raisins" and "Ebony Toothpaste with Green Fluoride Flecks." I put them next to my shopping list.

A corner of what appeared to be a coffee coupon peeked at me from the far edge of the cabinet. I jumped in the air and grabbed it. Well, the other end of the coupon, unknown to me, was tucked under the can of Crisco and out it tumbled. Practically before my feet hit the floor, the Crisco hit my head. I fell to the floor in agony.

More unfortunate, the Crisco was the main gate behind which hundreds of coupons were tossed. I was soon buried in an avalanche of from "5 cents" to "a dollar off." But this wasn't what almost killed me.

I barely escaped with my life when the very clever "razor blade coupon clipper" sliced its way into the linoleum, an eighth of an inch from my wrist.

I'd like to say this was the end of coupons in my life, that I scooped them up, tossed them in the waste basket (clever organizers and all), and declared a life-long moratorium on them.

But the truth is, coupon mania wins again. The clipper was not only right at my fingertips, but had landed next to the best two-for-one in the bunch.

The Big Mean Cleaning Machine: My Transformation into a Domestic Artist

Lynn Bowen Walker

The cleaning fairy does not live at our house. When my husband and I first got married, it took us a while to comprehend this. Clothes thrown on the floor just stayed there. Forever. Empty glasses with milk scum at the bottom didn't magically disappear from the nightstand.

Our mothers gleefully agreed we deserved each other.

In the beginning, this was not a problem. Equally oblivious to the crumbs on the counters, it appeared we were tailor-made for each other.

But one day all that changed. Our house was burglarized and—I'm not making this up—it took us an hour and a half to notice. I thought it was funny. But Mark? Well, from that day on he determined to mold me into the homemaker of his dreams.

Suddenly, he began notifying me of all elderly vegetables

residing in refrigerator compartments. He'd spot errant mail order catalogues offering personalized dog dishes, scattered throughout the house. Not that he did anything about said items, mind you, he just wanted to make sure I knew they were there.

Unfortunately, being receptive to well-intentioned advice has never been one of my strong points. But determined to place the role of loving wife and helpmeet at the top of my priorities—plus I didn't want to flunk the latest magazine marriage quiz—I knew the time was right for a change.

I read the verses about submitting to one another and considering others more important than yourself. If spanky clean was important to my husband, I figured spanky clean had better become important to me.

My well-thought-out plan for mending my ways (if not my mending pile) was based on rock-solid, scientific data: I would clean house the way they did on television commercials. The ladies on TV turned grease and grime into sparkly shine simply by donning their cutest size 2 outfits and beaming at a 1-gallon jug of pine cleaning solution.

That's it! I needed to buy some of that pine solution!

I returned from the supermarket staggering under the weight of spray bottles. My husband, pleased with my progress, added a huge dust mop to my supplies. My cleaning problems, I was convinced, were over.

Two years later, when it was time to move into our next home, I boxed up the virgin mop and all those (still) brand-new cleaning supplies. The horrible truth hit me: In order for the cleaning supplies to work, someone had to actually use them.

This was momentarily discouraging. But I quickly moved to the next stage in my cleaning metamorphosis. If I could find the

right book, the one that revealed what you actually do with the sudsy ammonia, surely then the cleaning fairy would flutter her wings and alight in my living room to live with us forever more.

I headed for the bookstore and brought home an armload.

By this time we had a couple of toddlers underfoot, which made the goal of transforming our home into a place of order and beauty a tad bit stickier (literally). But the books contained some valid direction nonetheless—at least they did once I unearthed them from beneath the piles of clean, folded laundry to be put away; clean, unfolded laundry to be folded and put away, and dirty laundry to be washed, dried, folded, and put away.

To start with, make lists of chores that need to be done (4,123 by my count), time available for cleaning each day (3 minutes, 17 seconds), then buy a three-ring binder, color-coded index cards, and a peppy little apron.

What you do with the cards and the apron I don't know, because this is where I tossed the books and began looking for a more palatable solution, one that didn't involve adding clammy yellow gloves to my everyday attire. After I considered several more theories, including my personal favorite that insisted messy people aren't lazy but merely perfectionists gone awry, my husband spoke up.

Being receptive to well-intentioned advice has never been one of my strong points.

"Instead of reading about vacuuming," he said, straining not to sound peevish, "why don't you just vacuum?"

I won't go into my immediate response (something about his hands fitting around the vacuum handle as well as mine). But I couldn't shake the nagging feeling he might be on to something.

The grand cleaning experiment began.

Toothpick in hand, I picked at the bolts that keep my toilet fastened to the floor.

I tried different strategies as I worked. I listened to books on tape to ease the monotony. I used a timer to keep myself going for short bursts. I started inviting company over more often, finding humiliation-avoidance to be an excellent motivator. I stopped allowing my house to become the junk mail in-box of the world. (Not to cast murky aspersions on Ed McMahon's character, but I'm relatively certain that when he claims that YOU, [FILL IN NAME HERE], ARE THE NEXT MILLION DOLLAR SWEEPSTAKES WINNER!!!, he is lying.)

I tried applying to my closets the verse that there's "a time to keep and a time to throw away" (Ecclesiastes 3:6b). I reminded myself, "A slothful man does not roast his prey, but the precious possession of a man is diligence" (Proverbs 12:27). I certainly did not wish to be caught prey-less come roasting time.

Slowly, gradually, I began to notice a change. There was a kitchen table in our kitchen! Once it was cleared, we could even eat on it!

As I kept at it, unearthing more exciting discoveries by the month, a strange, unfamiliar atmosphere of peace began to emerge in our home. Perhaps tidying and putting away wasn't so much bondage to chores as I had feared. Perhaps it actually represented freedom—freedom to enjoy my home and family and to find a pencil with a point when I needed it.

No one will ever mistake my home for the national institute of perfect order. Despite my best efforts I am not the cleaning fairy, and never will be. (You don't expect a fig tree to produce cherries, do you?) But as I've been willing to go down that painful path of change, seeking to learn from others, attempting to be diligent in my work at home, accepting my nature bent toward creativity yet never giving up hope for a more orderly existence, an amazing thing has happened.

I've become a good (OK, OK, passable) homemaker. Crumbs that once would have littered the counter until leap year now glare like a neon sign. Seems there's no going back.

And my husband, the one who instigated all this? He is thrilled at the progress. In an effort to do his part he's discovered his hands fit around the handle of a vacuum cleaner just fine.

And you ought to see that man with a squeegee.

If Mr. Clean Calls, Tell Him I'm Not In!

Martha Bolton

I hate housework. I only do it when it's absolutely necessary—like when I can't find one of the kids. Or when the floral pattern on my bedsheets starts taking root.

There are other signs I watch for that let me know it's time to clean the house. For instance, when I find snow at the top of my dirty clothes pile, I know wash day is at hand. Or when a rude guest signs in on my coffee table with her fingers, I concede it might be time to drag out the Pledge. And when my Airwick Solid melts 15 minutes after I set it out. I figure it's probably trying to tell me something.

Yet, even though I'm the only woman in the world who owns a washing machine with a mildew cycle, I still realize housekeeping is a necessary part of life. Boarding up the shower is no way

to get rid of unsightly lime stains, and the dishwasher overflowing shouldn't be a prerequisite to mopping the kitchen floor.

It's just that I don't want to overdo it. You know, like those people whose houses smell of so much Lysol, every time you take a breath you disinfect your lungs. These people are so clean and tidy, you couldn't have archaeological digs on their dresser tops. They'd never have so many dishes on their kitchen sink they forget what color it is. And pest exterminators would never consider using their homes for training maneuvers.

I prefer to think the perfect housekeeper is someone who can strike a happy medium. It's like the old saying, "A home should be clean enough to be healthy, but dirty enough to be happy."

Or to put it another way. "Keep your floors clean enough to eat off of, but leave enough food there to make it worth your while!"

Chapter 3

Merry Perils of Motherhood

The real menace in dealing with a five-year-old is that in no time at all you begin to sound like a five-year-old.

—JEAN KERR

I'd Tell You Why Motherhood Makes Women Absentminded, but I Forget

Nancy Kennedy

I once read a magazine article about postpartum amnesia. It quoted experts as saying the reason motherhood makes women so absentminded has to do with the hormones oxytocin, estrogen, and thyroxine being out of whack. This makes sense when you're a new mother who can't remember her address without reading it off the mailbox or who mechanically puts the carton of ice cream in the file cabinet. Eventually the hormones level out. The problem of forgetting which breast you left off with the last time you nursed remedies itself when you get tired of being lopsided, and you learn to write your name on your hand to remind yourself who you are. But when your baby drives off to college in her new car, you really can't blame your postpartum anything on the fact that you still need a note to remind yourself to pick up the dry cleaning before the cleaners goes out of business.

I have my own theory concerning motherhood forgetfulness. I believe it's due to brain overload. Take the average mother of three children. Throughout the course of a day she has to know who goes to what school, who needs lunch money and who hates cafeteria macaroni and cheese, who has soccer practice on Field B, and whose practice is at the elementary school. She has to know that Daughter A needs a pair of black tights for dance class, Daughter B has a teeth cleaning appointment at 4:30, the chicken needs to go in the oven at 4:15, and there's no toilet paper in the hall bathroom. She maintains the supply of trash bags, razor blades, and Band-Aids, knows that canned goods are at least five cents cheaper at Store X than Store Y, and has everyone's social security number, shoe size, and Christmas list memorized.

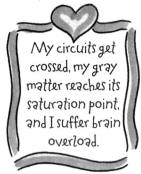

My circuits get crossed, my gray matter reaches its saturation point, and I suffer brain overload.

A few years ago when I went to a five-day conference, Barry took time off from work to be Mr. Mom. Before I left, I wrote out a list of everything that had to be done: Pick Laura and her friends, Kelly and Melanie, up from school at 2:55 (park on the left side facing east); then drop Melanie off at her brother's day care; then take Kelly home; then pick Alison up at 3:10 (park on the street by the cafeteria). Laura has cheerleading practice at five, and Alison needs to be at work at five, so take Alison first, etc., etc.

You get the picture.

Later, when I called home, Barry wailed into the phone, "You wouldn't believe all the things I had to do today!" Then he counted off about five of the more than twenty (bare minimum)

things I had listed. And forget about cooking; he ordered pizza all five nights I was away.

As forgetful as I am, I didn't forget to remind him I do all that (and then some) every day…without crib notes.

The daily routine stuff I rarely forget, but if you add a new variable (such as having to pick someone up at a later time), my circuits get crossed, my gray matter reaches its saturation point, and I suffer brain overload.

To remedy the situation, and to keep brain seepage to a minimum, I've devised a selective forgetfulness plan. For example: there are several things I plan to forget one day, such as the time a family member (who shall remain anonymous) took a piece of bread and wiped spaghetti sauce off her face—then ate the bread. "People sop up sauce on their plate," she reasoned. "Why not sauce on the face?"

I plan to forget the time I permed my hair a bit too tightly. Nobody said anything until a little girl in church turned around, looked at me, and announced, "Look, Mommy! That lady looks like Grandma's poodle!"

I plan on forgetting the words to every Raffi song ("Goin' on a picnic, leavin' right away; if it doesn't rain…"), every knock-knock joke ("Knock-knock. Who's there? Boo. Boo Who? Aww, don't cry."), every episode of *Full House.*

In a few years, I'll no longer remember how to do "My-mother-your-mother-lived-across-the-street…" hand clapping games or that Malibu Barbie gets the hot pink bathing suit and Superstar Barbie gets the evening gown. I won't even remember whether or not Sam I Am likes green eggs and ham.

Some things, though, are indelibly etched in my memory. I will never forget wheeling four-year-old Alison down the

crowded pet supplies aisle when she sighed (loudly) and asked, "Mom, do we *have* to eat dog food again tonight?"

I'll also never forget how she cured me (temporarily) from complaining about doing laundry. After about seven years of hearing, "All I ever do is laundry around here!" Alison devised a way to ease my load: she'd throw her underwear away instead of putting it in the hamper. However, there was one flaw in her logic, which she discovered after about a week when she went to get dressed for a Brownie field trip.

Around seven one Saturday morning, she came into my room and told me she didn't have any underwear.

"That's ridiculous," I replied. "Everyone in this family has underwear."

She looked at me and said, "I don't."

"Well, what happened to it?"

"I don't know."

"Did you have any yesterday?"

"Yes."

"What happened to those?"

"I don't know."

This line of questioning went on until I decided to search the house myself. Sure enough, she was right: no underwear any-where. And she had to get dressed and to her Brownie outing by 9:30.

After repeatedly urging her, "Come on, I won't get mad—just tell me where your underwear went," I finally got Alison to confess.

We got the story out in the open and I kept my promise not to get mad, but that didn't change the fact that she still didn't have any underwear to wear (except for the pair she'd thrown away the night before). We dug that pair out of the trash with the

plan that I'd wash them in the sink and put them in the dryer so Alison could be ready in time.

I thought it was a foolproof idea; I didn't count on the dryer conking out.

I went to Plan B.

I remembered my mom used to take our wet shoes and put them in the oven to dry off. I figured: *Shoes—underwear, what's the difference?*

I preheated the oven to 350 degrees, spread out her panties on a cookie sheet, set the timer for twenty minutes, then went to get myself dressed.

Twenty minutes passed. *Ding!* The timer went off, Alison and I raced into the kitchen, and she asked, "Are they dry, Mom?" I lifted up the charred remains (the rest having crumbled on the floor).

Our eyes grew wide and our mouths dropped open as we stared at Fruit of the Loom dust all over the kitchen.

"Yep," I told her. "They're dry."

I ended up driving all over the county for the next hour, trying to find a store that sold little girls' underwear that was open on a Saturday morning. We found one at nine, Alison made it to her Brownie outing in time, and from then on, I've used cookie sheets only for baking cookies.

Yes, because I'm a mother, my brain hovers dangerously close to overload; however, I'll always have room to remember these things:

- God's grace is amazing and sufficient for my every need. I'll never forget our year of unemployment when I was pregnant with Laura. In ways we still don't understand,

God allowed us to pay all our bills and still have money left over.

- The same power God used to raise Christ from the dead is available to me through the indwelling Holy Spirit (Ephesians 1:18ff). Although tired, I still manage to survive sleepless nights and function the next day. When sick myself, I've been able to nurse other family members who were down with the flu. This power enables me to stretch and bend in ways I never thought possible. It enables me to endure the times a child screams, "I hate you!" and to stand firm in my discipline. It enables me to live a life of holiness.

- I am created for God's glory (Isaiah 43:7) and for His pleasure (Revelation 4:11 KJV). He takes great delight in me, quiets me with His love, and rejoices over me with singing (Zephaniah 3:17). Whenever past failures haunt me or I'm overcome by fears of the future, I think of God singing because of me and am encouraged. His love lifts me and casts out all my fear.

- Someday I shall see Jesus.

Oh…and one last thing:

- Underwear is better air-dried than charbroiled.

Our Father, Who Art in Heaven —Hurried Is My Name

Nancy Chapman Monroe

Our Father, Who Art in Heaven—
Hurried is my name
I confess to a nagging feeling, Lord
That I'm not who I claim.

Honestly, Lord—this "do unto others" business
Sometimes does me in—
For while I'm really good at starting things
I seldom see the end!

For instance, there in a dusty heap
In the basket beside my chair
Lies a partially finished baby quilt
Right where I left it there.

I so admired the pattern;
I began with objective clear.
Too bad it will never keep the baby warm
He turned 21 this past year.

Now I try to keep my obligations;
I want so badly to please.
I try to serve on all committees
Where they need my expertise.

The principal calls to ask a favor;
The preacher calls me too!
I'm just the one they need, they say—
Nobody else will do!

So I buckle in and drive really fast,
Breathless all the way
I can't be late! But alas I find—
The meeting—it was yesterday!

My mind may be gone for good, Lord,
It's a bit too soon to tell
But they say that good intentions
Pave the road to—*welllllllll!*

So just for awhile Lord, if you don't mind
While I'm raising my family, don't you see
Do you think that you'd have the time
To take over and run the world for me?

Because despite all that I can do
I just can't win this game
I'm pedaling as fast as I can, Lord—
And hurried is my name.

College-Bound Kids Empty Our Nest

Marti Attoun

With two kids moving into college dorms, I'm feeling weepy and looking as pathetic as the "Homeless Pet of the Week."

It's not empty-nest syndrome. It's the larval stage of that affliction: plundered-nest syndrome. My daughter packed up the only hair dryer, hair curlers, and hand mirror in the house. I have a unibrow, but no tweezers. I have a bleak pallor, but no blush.

Every time I look around, I miss my grown-up kids—or my alarm clock, spare hangers, AA batteries, calculator, laundry detergent, or stash of Dr. Pepper.

I should have prepared for this. I should have bought the 24-pack of toilet paper on sale for $4.99. I should have socked away a spare toenail clipper. I should have known my duo would pack in laundry baskets and leave me wandering around the house with armloads of unfolded clothes.

"Is this the best we can do for towels?" their father asked as he fished a bleach-bitten scrap from my arms.

I nodded toward the paper towels.

"Get used to it," I said. "Your sock drawer has been liquidated, too."

An eerie quiet swamps the house. That's because our son took one TV, and our daughter took the other, leaving us with a crotchety black-and-white with rabbit ears. It can't hold a channel, but makes a dandy flat surface for holding other stuff, such as laundry.

It's amazing what simple acts can trigger the pangs of plundered-nest syndrome. For example: having to substitute a pair of underwear for a missing shower cap, or having to thread an ugly orange extension cord through two rooms to substitute for a missing power strip.

As I replenish the nest with microwave-safe dishes, spare pillows, and such, I remind myself that time will ease the sting of plundered-nest syndrome.

I hope it happens before the little darlings pop back home for a visit and find something else—such as the coffee pot or this computer—to cart away.

Chapter 4

Of Moms and Words

A little boy ran to his mother, "Mom! You know that antique clock of ours that has been passed from one generation to another?"

"Yes," the mother anxiously responded. "What's wrong?"

"My generation just dropped it!"

—STAN TOLER

Ask Me No Questions...and I'll Be Eternally Grateful

Nancy Kennedy

You know how it is. You think it's so incredibly cute when your little one asks, "Who made my nose? Who made my feet? Who made the dog's feet?" You even think it's unbelievably adorable when that same little one asks, "Does God have a beard?" and "Did Jesus eat hot dogs?" You may even think it's enormously enchanting when that child asks his grandfather, "Grandpa, if man was made in God's image, does that mean he has hair in his ears like you do?"

However, no matter how you do the math, cute, adorable, enchanting questions twelve thousand times a day times nineteen years equals fried eggs for brains.

My personal least favorites include the entire Why series and all its derivatives ("Why is the grass green? Why do I have five fingers? Why don't cows meow? Why can't I go downtown and

play Silly String cars with all my friends and stay out until after midnight? Why does your head look like it's going to fly off into outer space any minute?").

Tied with the Why series is the silly, mindless, endless What Ifs that are popular with five-and six-year-olds ("What if this bowl of cereal was really dog food and when people ate it they turned into dogs, and then what if the dogs all got together and they all turned into pianos? What if the ocean was made out of grape Kool-Aid and birds drove tractor trailers and ate bologna sandwiches? What if you rode a toilet to school and your name was Burp Burp?").

What Ifs are the older child's version of Hypothetically Speaking.

A sub-category of the endless What Ifs are the older child's version of Hypothetically Speaking, of which Laura reigns as Hypothetical Queen. These questions usually involve a potentially important (i.e., costly) piece of information wrapped in an innocent-sounding query. For example: "Hypothetically speaking, what happens to carpeting when red food coloring is spilled on it?" or, "Hypothetically speaking, what would happen if someone accidentally put pork chop bones down the garbage disposal, and how much would it cost to fix it?"

I thought I'd reached my limit shortly after the hypothetical pork chop incident (which, for further hypothetical information, costs $157.39 to fix). I called my mom and asked her, "Mom, do kids' questions ever go away? Do they ever stop? Is there any documented evidence of a woman's head exploding after listening to eight straight hours of, 'Why does Mickey Mouse have only four fingers?' and 'Why do people have earlobes?' Do they ever stop, Mom? Do they, huh? And what if…"

Mom laughed and told me, "No, the questions never stop; in fact, they get harder to answer."

She got that one right. They go from pointing to your nose and asking, "What zat?" to "How do I know if the Bible is true?" and "Is it really so wrong to have sex before marriage if the entire culture says it's right?" And in between they ask about earlobes and nose hair and why mommies shave under their arms and daddies don't.

Questions, questions. I'm constantly amazed that my kids think I know all the answers ("Mom, what exactly is thermodynamics, and how does it apply to my life?"). Just the other day Alison popped her head out of her room and asked, "Quick— Mom, what's an African animal that eats its young?"

The problem is, I know the answers, but they just don't ask the right questions.

I know that Albert Einstein's brain is stored in a Mason jar in Wichita, Kansas, and that it takes sixty chinchillas to make a chinchilla coat. I also know that the thing used to measure your feet in a shoe store is called a Brannock device. Of course, the most obvious response to that information is, "Who cares?" but that's not the point. The point is: I'm a fount of trivia tidbits, but normally no one bothers to ask me about such bits of tid and they seldom come up in everyday conversation. As a result, the girls' questions are usually met with a shrug of my shoulders and an "I don't know—go look it up."

I have questions of my own. Did Adam and Even have belly buttons? What do babies dream about? Is ear hair God's design or a result of sin? What ever happened to Charles Benson, and how can I thank him for telling me about Jesus way back in junior high school?

As a mother, I've wrestled with questions over movies that everybody else's mom says are OK and whether or not a sixth grader is old enough for an after-school dance. How do I know if I'm doing the right thing? How can I tell if I'm too strict or too lenient? What if my child chooses the wrong path in life? Can I stop her? Can I change her? Is it my fault?

Where's the line between helping a child and trying to live her life for her? Can a mother shoulder all her child's burdens? Should she? If not, how can she let go?

I've never gone to journalism school, but I do know that the cardinal rule for reporters is to go directly to the source with your questions.

God may not answer all my questions, and I'll probably have to wait until I get to heaven to find the answer about Adam and Eve's anatomy and the whereabouts of Charles Benson. But like a good parent, He'll tell me everything I need to know.

All I have to do is ask.

The Power of Words
Carol Kent

It was quiet in the house. Too quiet. Normally, four-year-old J. P. followed me from room to room. But I had gotten engrossed in a good book and suddenly realized I didn't hear his familiar noise. I panicked. How long had he been missing?

"Jason! Jason! Jason Paul Kent—where are you?"

No answer.

I quickly checked the kitchen, the bathroom, the living room and then dashed up the stairs to his room. At the time we were living in a unique old home with unusual architecture. The house had built-in cabinets, bookshelves, and closets everywhere—lots of places for a preschooler to hide. Running to J. P.'s room, I again called out, "Jason! Please answer me. Honey, *where are you?*"

I opened his closet door. In this rambling old house, J. P.'s closet had steps that led to the unfinished third-story attic. The

dust was thick up there, but the previous owner loved train sets, and he had built a huge track that encircled the entire perimeter of the third floor. The attic, with its unfinished wood, old nails, and precarious drop-offs, was a dangerous place for a four-year-old.

Normally, the attic was closed off, but J. P. claimed ownership of this special room with the secret entrance in his bedroom and referred to it as "*my* attic." He often begged to explore this forbidden, poorly ventilated room.

Breathlessly, I ascended the stairs to the attic hideaway and opened the door. My child was nowhere in sight. He had simply disappeared.

I called his name out again and again with no answer. I ran to my bedroom across the hall so I could telephone Gene and try to figure out what to do. I knew the police wouldn't come. He'd been missing such a short time. I was feeling desperate! As I grabbed the phone, I heard a sound coming from the closet in the master bedroom. I bolted across the room and opened the door.

There he was—seated on the floor of the closet. He had found a pair of my pantyhose and somehow managed to pull them on—over the top of both tennis shoes and over the top of his blue jeans. The waist of the pantyhose was right around his little belt. In retrospect, it was a very humorous sight, but laughter was *not* the first thought on my mind. He had deliberately chosen not to respond to my calls and had caused me severe anxiety.

He instantly recognized the irritated look on my face and before I could open my mouth, he looked deeply into my eyes, smiled, and with an innocent, pleading, high-pitched voice he said, "My legs are soft, Mom—just like yours!"

I realized that at four years old J. P. was already learning the power of using the right words to dissipate a tense situation.

When my birthday rolled around last April, J. P. forgot my special day. When his card arrived a week late, it pictured a shy little boy on the front with a sheepish grin, holding a card in his outstretched hand. I opened it up and the words before me read: "Will you forgive me for being late if I remind you of how cute I am?" Then in small print at the bottom of the card, he wrote, "Honest, Mom, you do not seem to have aged at all in my mind. Happy Birthday!"

Eviction Notice

Angela Elwell Hunt

Like most mothers, I nag my son for not keeping his room clean until I sound like one of those prerecorded voices you hear on airport shuttles. One day, however, I decided to try a creative approach to the problem. There would be no yelling, no threats, no flailing of arms.

When Eric came home from school, he found the following beautifully printed notice on his door:

Because the landlord entered these premises this
morning and found filth, mold, and carpet damage,
the tenant who inhabits this room is hereby

EVICTED
and all contents of this room
CONFISCATED

until further notice. Possession will be returned to tenant if the following conditions are met:

- A thorough cleaning of closet, space under bed, drawers, shelves, etc.
- Carpets shall be shampooed and scrubbed until stains are gone.
- All glasses and kitchenware are returned to kitchen and will NOT be allowed back into premises. Tenant shall not use model paints or glue in this space for a full six months.
- Until the above conditions have been met, tenant is not allowed inside the room except for the purpose of cleaning.
- Any supplies needed may be brought out by a parent or found in laundry baskets. Tenant may sleep in—but shall not mess up—the guest room.

While cleaning, tenant may not listen to CD player or bring out any possessions. This room is off limits until cleaned. Landlord shall, at her discretion, begin to discard any and all items found inside these premises if room is not cleaned before October 5, 1996.

Having a room of one's own is a privilege...and privileges can be revoked.

Respectfully yours,
The Management

I posted the eviction notice on a Wednesday morning. With church on Wednesday night, and after-school activities on Thursday and Friday, he didn't have an opportunity to clean his room until Saturday morning. Each night he slept in the spare bedroom

and the next morning he pulled his school clothes from the laundry basket. (I made sure there were clean clothes available.)

On Saturday, he got up and cleaned his room! Since then I've taken to calling Saturday "National Clean Your Room Day," and when Eric is slow to crawl out of bed, I just tell him he needs to get up and celebrate a national holiday. He understands what I mean—and the consequences of not listening—without my having to nag him.

Furry Fun

Your kids will feed their new puppy the day you buy it and the days you threaten to take it back to the pet store.

—BRUCE LANSKY

In the Company of Critters

Karen Scalf Linamen

Kacie loves critters.

In fact she loves animals of all kinds, including invisible ones.

Case in point: She's got this imaginary friend named Tito.

She began talking about Tito a couple years ago. Best we can tell, Tito is a dog. He also has a girlfriend named Marie.

Sometimes Tito has a bit of a mean streak. Like the time I was driving and looked into my rearview mirror and saw Kacie sitting quietly in her car seat, tears streaming down her face.

"Kacie! What's wrong?"

She blinked. "Tito bit me."

All our friends at church know about Tito. One man in particular enjoys teasing Kacie about Tito. Practically every time he sees Kacie, Herschel asks, "How's Tito?"

Sometimes Kacie tells him. Increasingly, however, Kacie merely crosses her arms and purses her lips as if to say, "Oh puh-lease, not again."

One day another friend overheard Herschel teasing Kacie. His curiosity piqued, Condall just had to ask, "Who in the world is Tito?"

Herschel told him.

Condall thought the whole thing was great and figured he'd get in on the fun. Squatting eye-level with Kacie, he grinned and said, "Hey Kacie, how's Tito?"

Kacie never even blinked. She eyeballed him back and said levelly, "Tito's dead."

So Herschel and Condall killed Tito. Tito stayed dead for several months until Marie managed to bring him back to life. Kacie explained that Marie did this with some sort of magic stones. I figured Kacie and Marie assumed this was safe to do because Herschel and Condall had finally stopped asking about Tito.

Tito was nowhere to be seen (which, come to think of it, is probably to be expected for an invisible dog).

Tito may have a mean streak, but he seems to appreciate his privacy.

When Kacie's not playing with invisible friends, the other critters she loves are garden critters. She's always begging me to help her find pill bugs, June bugs, crickets, even snakes.

She really loves the snakes. Little baby garden snakes. She gets this death grip around their little bodies and hangs on tight.

I always watch her closely when she's playing with snakes. I'm not worried about her physical safety as much as her psychological health. I don't think it's healthy for a child to have to live with the fact that she inadvertently squeezed the life out of a baby snake with her bare hands.

Besides, Kacie's probably already going to need therapy, what with having to kill Tito off like that.

In any case, the other day Kacie and I were wrapping up a day spent in the garden. Kacie had just spent the afternoon with many of her favorite critters. She had collected rollie pollies, chased crickets, prodded worms, studied ants, and befriended several moths.

It had been a well-populated afternoon, although if I remember right, Tito was nowhere to be seen (which, come to think of it, is probably to be expected for an invisible dog).

On our way inside for dinner, Kacie needled me with several dozen questions about worms and crickets and pill bugs and ants. I found myself explaining how all these critters and many others form a sort of community. I told her that the worms aerate the soil, and the bees pollinate the flowers, and the crickets…well, I don't really know what crickets do, but I'm sure I made something up and managed to sound fairly credible in the process.

I told her that each critter was important, and that our garden just wouldn't be the same without them all.

And I've been thinking about that conversation ever since.

I'm part of a community, too. I won't say if I'm more like the hardworking ant or the social butterfly (nectar, anyone?), but my point is that I am part of a community of critters, and every one of us has a unique role to fill. There are the quiet laborers, the encouragers, the movers and the shakers, the problem solvers and the huggers. In my community (as in yours, no doubt) there are even a few well-meaning pests.

What a privilege it is to have these folks in my life.

You know, the Bible encourages us not to forsake fellowship with other believers. I think it's because we really do need each other. Not a one of us can thrive isolated and on our own.

Not even Tito.

He might be a little shy around Herschel and Condall, but I hear he's sticking close to Kacie and Marie these days.

They knew right where to find those magic stones, after all.

Really, I'm Thinking of You
Marilyn Meberg

Our daughter, Beth, came tearing into the house one morning with a look on her seven-year-old face that meant *I have an idea too big for the universe!*

"Mama," she began, "we could have a horse! It could play in the backyard, drink from the swimming pool, and sleep in the garage. We have plenty of room. I just decided!" Whenever Beth "just decided" anything, it took a good bit of energy as well as creativity to move her away from her conviction.

She countered each of my arguments against a horse with the same statement, "My teacher says taking care of a pet helps ya learn 'sponsibility." Every now and then Beth would broaden her argument with, "I need to get that 'sponsibility sometime, ya know."

Ultimately, we worked our way down from a horse to a hamster. She reluctantly agreed one could learn 'sponsibility with a small animal just as well as with a large one. That issue settled, Beth and I went to the pet store, where she selected Sugar from a squirming throng of other hamsters. We also bought a Plexiglas cage, an exercise wheel, and special hamster food guaranteed to maintain Sugar's robust health.

Initially, the whole family took an active interest in Sugar, but her utter indifference to us squelched any anticipation we may have had of meaningful relatedness. After all, the whole purpose was to give Beth an opportunity to develop 'sponsibility.

Several weeks after Sugar became a family member, Beth announced she was sure Sugar was bored. We all felt slightly bruised. How could she be bored? She had a lovely cage, wheel, food, and all of us at her disposal should she want us.

Beth described a Plexiglas round ball that her friend Suzie had for her hamster. She put the hamster in the ball, snapped it shut, and the hamster simply roamed around the house in this little ball. When the hamster moved, the ball moved.

So, in an effort to relieve the tedium in Sugar's life, Beth and I once again headed for the pet store and purchased a roaming ball. I don't know who was more delighted with that ball, Sugar or me. We would put her in the ball, click it shut, and off she would go in a flash, bumping into furniture and walls, righting herself, and then speeding off in another direction. It was rather like watching a miniature bumper car on the loose.

What particularly gave me a giggle was guests' reactions as Sugar would flash through a room. A first-time visitor who caught a glimpse of this self-propelled, fur-filled ball moving rapidly and haphazardly through the house and then quickly disap-

pearing found the experience a bit unsettling. Ken and I often pretended we hadn't seen it and professed puzzlement as visitors tried to describe their sightings.

As Sugar's enthusiasm for her ball began to wane, we were all concerned she might be slipping back into her former state of boredom. Often we would find her in her ball dozing in a corner, behind a couch, or under a table. She made little effort to explore anymore. We knew, of course, that hamsters are nocturnal creatures and do most of their wild living at night, but, nonetheless, Sugar was exhibiting signs of lassitude. What could we do?

Beth suggested we buy Sugar a "sky restaurant." Suzie had purchased one for her hamster, and it had seemed to raise its flagging spirits considerably. We agreed that might be the answer for Sugar. Later, as I watched her zip up the little cylindrical tube that led to a separate floor, I wondered what would happen to her fragile psyche when she discovered that despite its name, food was never served up there in the sky restaurant's tower.

Predictably, the sky restaurant soon lost its appeal. That made perfect sense to me—the promise of food that never appeared would certainly put me in a slump. With some concern, we realized Sugar occasionally whiled away her time by gnawing on the far-right corner of her cage. It occurred to all of us she might be working on an escape route, but surely she couldn't gnaw through Plexiglas. Surely the best she could manage would be a dime-size opening.

One night around 2 A.M., I awakened to an odd noise. I poked Ken into startled awareness, and of course, he heard nothing. I lay

A first-time visitor who caught a glimpse of this fur-filled ball moving found the experience a bit unsettling.

there as he immediately fell back to sleep and ultimately decided he was right. It was nothing.

Then it sounded again. A hurrying, scurrying sound seemed to come from under the bed. It then trailed quickly to the dressing area and into the adjoining bathroom. I leaped out of bed, grabbed the flashlight, and beamed it into the bathroom. Sugar was staring back at me with her little cheeks and neck stuffed so full of something she was barely recognizable in her lumpiness. Carefully setting her and her cargo back in the cage (The top was off; how had that happened?), I watched with delight as Sugar proceeded to spew forth from her mouth one brightly colored wooden bead after another. The beads would hit the Plexiglas wall and then roll into silence. One, two, three, four, five, six…finally, seventeen beads later, little Sugar had disgorged her treasures.

"Try not to take it too hard. You did everything you could."

Apparently in her early-morning foray throughout the house, Sugar had discovered the beads under Beth's bed. (Beth and Suzie had been making necklaces to complement their second-grade wardrobes.) I scooped up the beads, thanked Sugar for a wonderful giggle, and went back to bed.

A few weeks later, I returned from work to discover Sugar had escaped again. She had gnawed through the cage corner and was nowhere to be seen. The slider screen to the backyard was slightly ajar, so I assumed she had ventured outside. But my searching was unsuccessful. This time she was gone for good.

When I told Beth about Sugar's escape, instead of the pained response I had anticipated, Beth was relieved. Her philosophical

response was, "That's probably best, Mama. Nothing seemed to maker her happy anyway." Noticing my lingering concern, Beth added, "Try not to take it too hard. You did everything you could." Several hours later, she followed me into my study and said, "Would a horse make you feel better?"

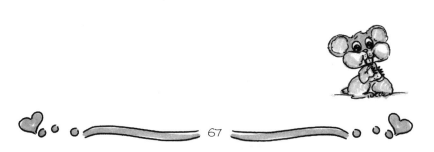

Who Loves Ya, Baby?

Karen Scalf Linamen

I eavesdropped on my five-year-old the other night.

She was all tucked into bed, waiting for me to come in and tell her a story, when she decided to sing herself a song.

I was in the hallway, approaching her bedroom door, when I heard the familiar words in her child's voice:

"Jesus loves me, this I know, for the Bible tells me so…"

I stopped in my tracks and listened, feelings of joy and gratitude welling up inside of me. This is because nothing blesses a mother's heart like witnessing her children engaging in true worship. I knew I was on hallowed ground as I observed a precious moment in my little one's relationship with her Creator.

Kacie sang for several minutes. Then she paused, regrouped, and began again. This time there was a slight alteration in the words.

She exchanged "Jesus" for "Walter."

As in, "Walter loves me, this I know."

Walter is our German shepherd.

Okay, so it was still a nice moment, although I have to admit it left me with a few questions about Kacie's theology. One day soon, remind me to have a talk with Kacie about how God is different from a German shepherd.

Although, really, when you think about it, I guess I can't blame her. I mean, fully grasping what it means to be loved by Someone you can't see or touch is a pretty tough concept for a four year old.

It can be a tough concept to grasp even when you're forty.

Let's face it. When Walter loves you, you KNOW it. This is because even though Walter is only 7 months old and merely half of his adult weight, he has no shortage of energy and mass. At fifty pounds, he has a tendency to gallop through the house like a Shetland pony on Metabo-life.

And when Walter's feeling affectionate, watch out: He slobbers. He jumps and skids around on the kitchen linoleum. He flings his body, not unlike a heat-seeking missile, at any warm-blooded target in the room. He wags his tail so hard he's been known to send furniture and compact vehicles flying. In short, his affection is so tangible that it can put you in the hospital if you're not careful.

Then there's God, who is invisible and intangible and does not dispense bruises, saliva or dog hairs.

Have you ever wished God were a bit more tangible?

I have.

Ever wished you could see his face, hear his audible voice, feel his arms around you?

Me too.

In fact, I was feeling that way just last Sunday. Had a bad week and was apparently wearing it on my face, because my friend Kathy Clegg came up to me and said, "How are you doing?"

And I could tell she really wanted to know.

"Not good," I said.

"I know. I can tell. You look like you need a hug." And she hugged me.

The truth is, I've had some struggles in my life the past year or so, and I've been blessed to have some really wonderful friends rally around me. They don't always agree with me, or condone everything I think or say or do, but they've been loving me nonetheless with their smiles and their words and their hugs.

And in the process, well, a sort of magic has been occurring as the invisible, intangible God has been showing up in my life in a visible, tangible manner.

How do I know this is happening?

For starters, he just feels closer, which is nice—I certainly won't knock it—but the real proof is in the pudding, as it's written in 1 John 4:11–12. These verses say, basically, "Dear ones, if God loved us THIS much—enough to send his Son Jesus into the world to pay the price for our wrongdoings—then we should love each other. It's true that no one has ever seen God, but if we love each other, God dwells in us."

If we love each other, the Invisible dwells in us. God shows up. He's there. He's present. On top of all that, his love isn't intangible at all, not when it's being lived out through flesh-and-blood friends who are ready and willing to dispense hugs, help-

ing hands, chicken soup, carpool favors, greeting cards, good advice, and even a shoulder to cry on.

You want a tangible God? Then get vulnerable with huggable friends who have Jesus living in their hearts. Best yet, you won't have to brush dog hairs off your clothes.

Chapter **6**

Caution: Mother on the Loose

Q: What is the most common pregnancy craving?

A: For men to be the ones who get pregnant.

—LOWELL D. STREIKER

Stuck Where I Did Not Belong

Lynn Assimacopoulos

One day when I was pregnant with our first child, I went shopping at a large department store downtown. Eager to buy my first maternity outfit, since I was not fitting very well into anything else anymore, I headed straight for the maternity department. I wasn't exactly very big yet, just big enough not to fit in regular clothes. I began trying on maternity clothes, which in those years were always two-piece. (Funny no one had yet figured out how ugly they were and that it would be much better to make one-piece outfits.) I tried on several outfits in the "fitting" room, then went out to the three-way mirror to see how each one looked. What a sight! Not pregnant enough to show, but desperate enough to need to buy something. I looked like someone who could not tell what size to buy. The outfits were like tents and swished around my body like waves of cloth not quite sure where to go.

During one trip, as I attempted to retreat back to the fitting room, I was met by several young women in three-inch heels going the opposite direction. I tried to fight my way back to the fitting room, but for some reason they were in a very big hurry and being much taller, paid no attention to me. (I thought I was tall at five feet and five inches, but these woman seemed to be at least six feet tall since I remember looking straight into jewelry,

I had been mobbed by department store models into a fashion show area.

furs and fancy dresses instead of seeing any faces.) I also remember smelling lots of perfume. They just kept on coming and I was forced to join them going in the opposite direction out some kind of exit into the middle of a circle shaped area. When the bright spotlights hit me in the face, I realized that I had been mobbed by a bunch of department store models into a fashion show area. And there I was in those awful maternity clothes staring straight into the crowd under a spotlight! Mortified? Yes! Almost to the point of nausea. Thank heaven *that* did not happen.

You have never seen a pregnant woman exit so fast back to the fitting room, where I stayed for a very long time, until I was certain that the fashion show was over, not wanting to show my face or my pregnant body again.

I think sometimes that happens to all of us. We get pushed and shoved where we really do not belong. Stuck in the wrong line or in the wrong situation. Following the crowd, going in the opposite direction that we want to. Others looming tall over us

and carrying us right along with them into an unknown situation. Stuck at a distance from God. Wondering if He has abandoned us and why. Thinking that His word and promise doesn't seem to fit at the moment. And when we actually see where we are headed and realize what is happening, we have to struggle and push and shove our way back to where we really belong. And maybe even hide out until things blow over. It can be done no matter how mortified or ugly we feel. We can always sneak back and wait until we can emerge safely once again. But we need a lot of help from God. And He is always there beside us, willing and able to help us with the correct "fit," the correct direction and the correct path to Faith.

I Don't Care How Famous You Are: I'm STILL Your MOTHER!

Becky Freeman

PAUL REVERE'S MOTHER: "I don't care where you think you have to go, young man, midnight is past your curfew."

MONA LISA'S MOTHER: "After all that money your father and I spent on braces, that's the biggest smile you can give us?"

COLUMBUS'S MOTHER: "I don't care what you've discovered, you still could have written!"

MICHELANGELO'S MOTHER: "Can't you paint on walls like other children? Do you have any idea how hard it is to get that stuff off the ceiling?"

NAPOLEON'S MOTHER: "All right, if you aren't hiding your report card inside your jacket, take your hand out of there and show me."

ABRAHAM LINCOLN'S MOTHER: "Again with the stovepipe hat? Can't you just wear a baseball cap like the other kids?"

MARY'S MOTHER: "I'm not upset your lamb followed you to school, but I would like to know how he got a better grade than you."

ALBERT EINSTEIN'S MOTHER: "But it's your senior picture. Can't you do something about you hair? Styling gel, mousse, something...?"

GEORGE WASHINGTON'S MOTHER: "The next time I catch you throwing money across the Potomac, you can kiss your allowance good-bye!"

JONAH'S MOTHER: "That's a nice story. Now tell me where you've really been for the last three days."

THOMAS EDISON'S MOTHER: "Of course I'm proud that you invented the electric light bulb. Now turn it off and get to bed."

How My Son Saved Easter

Lynn Bowen Walker

It was with high hopes last Easter that I whipped together a batch of homemade salt dough, ready for the hours of fun family time with my children that would result. As I mixed, cooled, and kneaded, I imagined our cozy family of four all scooched up close around the round kitchen table (never mind that ours is rectangular), laughing together as we fashioned little clay shapes that would become an Easter centerpiece. Of course, it would be identical to the picture in the craft book—a delicate bird's nest cradling tiny blue robin's eggs.

In this picture in my head we were each doing our small part. My boys were squishing dough through the garlic press in a beautiful cooperative effort. My husband and I were gently extracting every ounce of teachability from the moment. I envisioned how we would talk about working together as a body,

each one with his unique role that added up to a perfect whole. We might talk about the symbolism of the eggs as new life, or the nest and the way God can make something useful and good out of the scruffy, old twigs in our lives. Oh, the fun we would have!

"Hey guys," I hollered up the stairs. "Come on down. I have a project for us to do."

Over the background noise of incessantly cheery video game music, I distinctly heard groans. "Do we have to?" said one of the boys, or maybe it was both.

I searched my brain for an answer. This wasn't in my script.

"Well, no, you don't have to," I stammered. "But it'll be fun. We're going to make an Easter centerpiece." My enthusiasm began to wane as my fantasy family was slowly replaced by my real one. Without wanting to, I recalled my last attempt at family crafts time. Or maybe it was the last dozen attempts. Into my memory came the beautiful origami paper that I finally conceded would never be folded into little paper cranes (we sold the paper at the church flea market). Next came the cross-stitch kits I had poignantly passed on to two young girls last summer, finally acknowledging that we were not to be a cross-stitch family, either. To my dismay, the memories just kept coming.

"Guys? What do you say?" My 12- and 13-year-old sons are kind and sensitive and all that, but the choice between Crash Bandicoot video games or a spiritually significant craft project with Mom was a no-brainer.

"Uh, Mom? Mind if we don't come?"

"No," I faltered. "But if you change your mind…it's gonna be fun." I sounded lame even to myself.

My husband was happy in the garage doing chores, so I decided to make the nest and eggs myself. It *would* be fun. They'd see.

A couple hours later I had my centerpiece. Not precisely like the picture in the book, but close enough. I called my friend, a kindergarten teacher, to tell her about the project—at least someone cared—and even suggested it might work for her class. I went to bed a contented woman.

I should have known something was amiss when, in the middle of the night, the dog uncharacteristically whined to be let outside. Twice. When I got up the next morning I was confronted with copious evidence, from the kitchen all the way through the living room, that she desperately needed to be let out not twice but three times. Apparently our furry friend had hoisted herself onto the kitchen table and chosen my salt dough masterpiece as her midnight snack. All that salt dough must have made her thirsty enough to drink buckets of water, which made her have to…well, you know.

After an emergency trip to rent a carpet steam cleaner, I was finally ready to give up. We were not a crafty creative family. And it looked like we would never be.

That night I tossed my mutilated nest and eggs into the garbage. A bit dejected, I pulled out the leftover dough from the refrigerator. I sat down and absentmindedly began squeezing it through my fingers; it was the perfect texture for squishing and squeezing. I pulled out some eggshells I had hollowed earlier in the week, back when my holiday fantasy was still in full force. I sat and waited for inspiration. It didn't come.

"Whatcha doin'?" asked one son on his way through the kitchen.

"Just trying to figure out what to do with this dough, and these eggs." No enthusiastic pitch for his participation. No craft book to wave at him. No agenda.

My son sat down and picked up some dough. "This stuff is neat." I looked up in surprise. He started twisting it into shapes. "We could put crosses in the eggs," he suggested. We tried it, sticking blobs of dough into the two-inch-long opening in the side of each egg, and carefully squishing in little dough crosses.

"How about if we twist the different colors of dough together and put the little rope around the eggshell openings?" I suggested, and we did.

"Let's make a base," my son added, fashioning more dough into a rectangular block. "The eggs could go on top."

"Yeah," I said, picking up on his enthusiasm, "we have three eggs, just like the three men who were crucified together, Jesus and the two thieves." We set the three eggs on the base. Next we made a cave of dough to represent Christ's tomb, and as a final touch, we set a stone next to it to signify the stone that was rolled away.

> A good hour had passed with the two of us working side by side, laughing, talking, bonding.

We stepped back to admire our creation. A good hour had passed with the two of us working side by side, laughing, talking, bonding.

"This is really neat," my son said.

"Yeah," I agreed, meaning more than just the new centerpiece.

The world stopped for a few minutes as we stood gazing at our Easter scene, my arm around my son's shoulder. That moment I was struck anew with God's glorious grace, how he cared enough to take the efforts of an overzealous mom, an apathetic family, and a gluttonous dog, and somehow create something wonderful.

Maybe I couldn't turn us into a picture-perfect family with scripted roles and scripted lines.

Maybe I should stop trying. Maybe this real family—and the unexpected special moments given to us by a loving heavenly father—was even better.

If you're thinking of making an Easter centerpiece of your own, try it, it's fun.

But watch the dog.

Chapter 7

The Joys of Parenthood

My mother finally admitted in her later years that the easiest way for her to get me to do something was to forbid me to do it.

—GENE PERRET

Haircut Wars

Charlene Ann Baumbich

I t started with Bret when he was three years old, this thing about hair. Up until then, it was just something that grew on his head. Oh sure, we'd had an occasional bout of entangled gooey gum wads, but other than that, hair was just something that basically took care of itself after a little washing and slicking down.

Then one day hair issues as we knew them changed.

Bret sat watching early Saturday morning cartoons—with the scissors. This was, obviously, an activity he had not checked in with Mom about. I walked around the corner just in time to see disaster strike. He had the scissors laid flat to his scalp on the very top of his head. The hinge rested just at the hairline of his forehead. The blades were open, as was his mouth. Before I could open mine, *CRUNCH!*

The scalping registered in my brain in slow motion. His

trance-like state seemed to have nothing to do with the rest of his body. It was as though his arm and hand had acted on their own.

"Bret!" I screamed, but of course too late. I responded more to the horror of what had already happened than in warning. Two-inch, slick brown hairs slid down past his eyes and over his nose.

"Bret!" I repeated. "What have you done?"

"Nothing."

"Oh yes you have, you've cut a path down the top of your head!"

"No I didn't," he said, brushing the itchy telltale remnants out of his face.

"Go look in the mirror."

He strolled into the bathroom, pulled out the stool from under the sink and hopped up to mirror height. A look of terror captured his face and stayed there, thereby confirming my suspicions that his arm and hand had indeed acted on their own accord.

"My gosh, Bret, you're gonna have to get a crew cut to even that out. It's right smack down the middle!"

"I don't want to get a crew cut," he said, seeming surprised at the suggestion.

"Well, let's see what we can do then, if anything." I wet his hair and tried combing it this way and that. No matter what I did or how sopping I got it, it still wanted to flop apart at its man-made, one-inch-wide part. The fact Bret had slicker-than-slick, straight-as-a-board brown locks that always fell into bangs, no matter what, didn't help either.

"Well, I don't see much choice. Let's go into town and let the barber have a look to see if he has any suggestions." Bret wanted

to try fixing it for himself first. I handed over the comb. Then the brush. He finally gave up. Off to town we went.

The barber made the mistake of laughing when Bret walked in the door. I must admit, it was obvious why we were there, but Bret is a sensitive person. He was embarrassed, to say the least.

After setting him up in the chair, draping him with the striped cloth, turning him from side to side and whipping the remaining hair around a few times, the barber said there was only one alternative: crew cut. So be it. Closer to scalped was more the truth, but calling it a crew cut sounded better.

"It'll grow back soon," I said in consolation to a sick-looking little boy.

Well, Bret's hair doesn't grow very fast. It's the only time in his life he has ever worn a baseball cap with regularity.

But hair has that wonderful way of giving one perspective: it will always grow back. No matter how terribly it's cut, colored or permed, you can always grow a fresh crop.

Yes. Perspective. A straightforward look at the reality of the situation. The notion that this, too—whatever it is—shall probably pass. It isn't usually, after all, life-threatening.

Consider all the options and outcomes. Is it something to find the funny side in, or something you should stop laughing about? Pondering the worst-case scenarios can often produce livable solutions. Bounce it off someone else. Stand back and take in the big picture. A good hair story does wonders for my perspective. How about you?

Summer Commandments

Joey Earl Horstman

You may freely climb of the climbing tree of the lawn; but of the other trees you may not climb. You may not climb of the apple tree or of the maple tree or of the cottonwood tree or of the willow tree, or of any of the bushes of the lawn, for in the day that you climb of them they will die. Of all but the climbing tree you are forbidden. Lo, you will be tempted to climb of the other trees, but climb them not, nor hang from their limbs, nor strip the bark from their trunks. For my eyes will be open, and I will call unto you, and you will be sorely afraid.

Bonk not your brother with the tennis racket, lest you be bonked. Again I say, bonk not. Though your brother's head doth appear as a tennis ball, and his taunting has made you angry, yea, even to the nth degree, bonk not his head with the racket, nor

roll him down the hill when he does not want to roll, nor use him as second base, nor tie him to the fence post with your jump rope. He is your brother. Afflict him not.

Your friends will say unto you, "Leave your toys on the driveway and play in the lawn with us"; but I say to you, leave not your toys on the driveway. Pick up in the garage that I may drive the minivan into it. Your roller skates and baseball bats, your Hotwheels cars and bicycles, yes, even your wagon, pick them up, I say, for do they not also have a selected place to be?

Keepest thou not the refrigerator door open, for that is an abomination to me. Decide what you want before the opening of it, be it juice of a pear or a carrot. If you cannot decide, and are sorely confused, open it not. Do not open the refrigerator door and then stare inside, for it is as if you stare inside for hours. Verily, I say unto you, "Am I made of money?"

Throw not the baseball at the picture window, nor the soccer ball, nor the basketball, nor the football, nor any ball of the air or rock of the ground. For the glass it doth break and shatter from its holding and causeth thy mother great suffering. Throw not, and you shall not be thrown into time-out.

Tattle not on thy brother. Again I say, tattle not, for it is as if you tattle all the time. If your brother calls you out when you are safe, scream not for your father who art mowing, for he cannot hear you and has turned his face from you. If your brother squirts you with water when you do not wish to be squirted, ask of him that it shall not be done again, but leave your father in the peace that passeth your understanding.

Mumble not under your breath when you walk away from me. Neither whine, nor slam your bedroom door, nor throw your

shoes across the living room even if you cannot have a cookie or cannot stay up past the appointed time of your bed. Why do you mumble so? Am I not your father, and can I not hear?

Eat not of the grass of the yard, nor of the dandelions, nor of any of the weeds we cannot identify and which will not depart from us. For doth not your parents feed you well and provide you with every good fruit and vegetable of the grocery store and garden? Ask and they will be given you. But eat not of the grass, lest you be sick and, being sick, make thy brother sick as well.

> Do not say that you have showered yesterday and need not shower today.

Touch not the poison oak, nor the poison ivy, nor rub your face with its leaves, for it will afflict you for seven days and seven nights. Red will be the color of your skin and in Aveeno will you bathe.

Of the number of showers you must take in a week, the number shall be four, for I am a clean father. Do not shower three times and claim that it was four, nor shower twice and claim that it was four. Do not say that you have showered yesterday and need not shower today, for that is a lie and you are not yet good at it. Shower four times, and soak thy head with soap and clean thy body, yes, even under the arms, for thy skin perspires and drives me from you.

Wear not those pants with that shirt. For the colors they do clash, and the stripes do not conform to the plaid. It pleases me not and hurts mine eyes to look upon you. Wear your underwear clean, and do not change it several times a day so that you have no underwear at the end of the week. Seven times shall you change, and the time of the changing shall be morning.

Giggle not when you are supposed to be sleeping, no, not

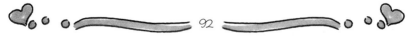

even if your brother tells a joke, for he is four and his jokes do not make sense anyway. Nor hidest thou Milk Duds under thy pillow to be eaten later, for the Duds they do melt and soil the sheet and the pillow case, yes, even thy hair. Sleep when it is time to sleep, and jump not on the bed, for it is as if you have ants in your pants. Your bed is bunked, and the ceiling is low, so jump not.

There is a time for everything, as you will know when you are wise: a time for playing on the playground and a time for feeding the dog; a time to be in the pool and a time to be on the land; a time to run and a time to sit still. Celebrate this time, for though the summer is long, it lasts not forever.

There's Still Room to Spare for My Son's Fashion Feats

Marti Attoun

Do you have enough wiggle room for your toes?" the shoe salesman asked my 12-year-old son as he test-walked and hopped in his pricey new sneakers. I wondered if I had enough wiggle room in my checkbook.

The salesman dug his thumb into the sneaker toe and calculated that there was a good "thumbnail's worth" of space. At the rate the kid's feet were growing, I calculated that he'd outgrow a thumb's worth after three more orders of spicy fries.

"Are they comfortable?" the salesman foolishly asked, as if comfort should be a criterion for shoe-buying at age 12.

My son nodded and stepped over the knee-high mirror to admire his footwear while coming, going and scooting sideways.

Finally, he gave a thumbs up.

"They're cool. I'll take these."

We'd already bought the trendy low-cut athletic socks, which barely peeked over the edge of the shoes. We called these "footies" in my day, when only matronly females wore them. The fancy ones had pastel rabbit tails bobbing at their heels. Still do.

Overnight, it seems that the kid has reached that finicky age where he's on full-time fashion alert and mortified by a father who stretches his own socks up to his knees and a mother who laughs about "footies."

"This is what golfers wear," he'd already informed me about the, uh, socks-in-training. "And, by the way, please don't talk so loud, Mom."

I whispered to him that my hearing was impaired after years of listening to his siblings' loud, obnoxious music.

Yes, he's growing up and galloping into teenhood, I thought during this shopping trip. We'd already combed the clothes racks for the must-have cargo shorts and T-shirts with the proper name brands.

Not so long ago, he'd wear anything I hung in his closet, even third-hand from a garage sale. Now, just the idea that his mother pokes through strangers' cast-off clothes and bud vases and such is enough to wreck his life forever.

In seventh grade, he's at that age where his father and I quickly are becoming ghost parents. Soon, he won't be able to see us or hear us in public. We'll call his name, but he'll look the other way. We'll be invisible, except for our glowing pockets.

I reached for my iridescent checkbook while the salesman boxed up his new sneakers.

Then the salesman stopped, lid in hand, and studied my son.

"If you want, I can pack up your old shoes, son, and you can wear these new shoes right now," he said.

"Yeah!" my son shouted.

Thank goodness we've still got a little wiggle room before he grows up completely.

Chapter 8

Mothering Rule #29: Embarrass Your Kids

I didn't make the same mistakes my parents made when they raised me. I was too busy making new ones.

—BRUCE LANSKY

Peculiar Purpose
Becky Freeman

One day I was driving down the road minding my own business when, a few cars ahead of me, I saw a grocery sack fall out of the back of a pickup truck. (In Texas, you're rarely more than a car's length from a pickup.) I could see that one of the items rolling out of the sack down the highway appeared to be a bottle of shampoo.

Then, like in one of those comical chase scenes in movies, the car in front of me ran smack over that shampoo bottle, whereupon it exploded, depositing its entire contents onto my windshield.

Gabe, my then ten-year-old son, was sitting in the front seat beside me. I glanced at him briefly. He said nothing, but his mouth was wide open and his eyes were darting back and forth from the windshield to me to see what I would do next. I

couldn't see a thing through the bluish green muck, so I turned on my windshield wipers.

At that very moment it started to rain. No kidding. So now I had this fascinating foaming bubble bath in full swing, sliding back and forth across my windshield. The more the wipers swept, the more the bubbles foamed and multiplied. Soap lifted off and floated from the car in streams as we drove along in the sudden shower. I glanced over at Gabe once again. Still no words coming from him, but his mouth was a little bit wider, and his eyebrows were so high they'd now disappeared under his bangs. We neared home, and as I pulled into the driveway, suddenly the sun burst from behind the clouds—the rain gone as quickly as it had begun. My windshield was sparkling clean. I rolled down my window, poked my head out, and looking up in the direction of the clouds said, "Thank you, Lord, You did a great job. I don't think my windshield's ever been this clean before."

Gabe finally found his voice, but when he did it was trembling. "Mo-o-o-m," he squeaked, "do you think other kids' mothers have these kinds of things happen to them?"

All I could do was smile and shrug, and assure him that some of us are called to be peculiar people walking through peculiar circumstances—so we can make other folks feel much better about their own lives.

Phone Etiquette Gets Ringing Disapproval
Marti Attoun

Sometimes I marvel at how I ever managed to grow up, dress myself, and get a job without advice from my kids.

My latest lesson came yesterday. I've been answering the telephone ever since our prefix was MAY-FAIR and Aunt Vera chatted on a party line, but I've been doing it all wrong.

"I know this is a fine point, Mom," my young-adult son began in all earnestness, "but never, ever, pick up the phone on the first ring."

What precipitated this teaching moment was a female caller (for him) on the other end of the line. I pounced on the phone because I was sitting at my desk and it was tolling two inches from my fingertips.

He sighed and patiently explained, "Mom, when you answer the telephone on the first ring, it immediately puts you under the

power of the other person. Do you want people to have that much power over you? It makes you look desperate, like you're sitting there waiting for that person to call."

But I am desperate and powerless when I'm waiting for a call from Jerry, the world's best air-conditioning guy. He has a waiting list longer than my ductwork, and I wouldn't dream of making either of us sweat an extra second.

> "You're getting a bite! You're getting a bite!" we yell whenever her phone line rings.

And, besides, it could be Mom who just tugged a blackberry cobbler out of the oven and wants me to fetch it. I have to grab that call and cobbler before one of my sisters picks up on their first ring.

Sometimes, I even answer the phone breathlessly. It doesn't mean that I'm panting over the caller. It means that I just wrenched a bundle of clothes out of the washing machine and ran up the basement steps.

I explained all of this to my son, but he still insisted that it shouted LOSER! when I picked up the phone on its first whine.

"If you want to learn how to use a telephone, Mom, take lessons from Abby," he said with pride about his sister. To this girl, a telephone is like a fishing pole.

"You're getting a bite! You're getting a bite!" we yell whenever her phone line rings.

If this were me, I'd reel it in immediately and see what's on the other end of the line.

Abby calmly checks her Caller ID/fish finder. If it's a rainbow trout, she picks up on the third nibble or so. If it's an unknown or a carp, he gets to talk to the answering machine.

I'm afraid that it's too late for me to rewire my telephone habits. When my phone rings, I'll continue to snatch it as swiftly as I can reach it. If I don't answer, it doesn't mean that I'm trying to act all powerful. It just means that the loser isn't home.

The Talk

Richard W. Bimler and Robert D. Bimler

There's a story about a sweet little girl who asks her daddy, "What's sex?" So her father sits her down and tells her all about conception, sperm and eggs, puberty, and many other aspects of sexuality. *After all,* he thinks, *let's tell everything since she has asked.*

The little girl is somewhat awestruck and bewildered. Her father finally asks, "So what made you ask about sex?"

"Oh, Mommy said lunch would be ready in a couple of secs…"

Chapter

9

Mothering Rule #30: Get Embarrassed by Your Kids

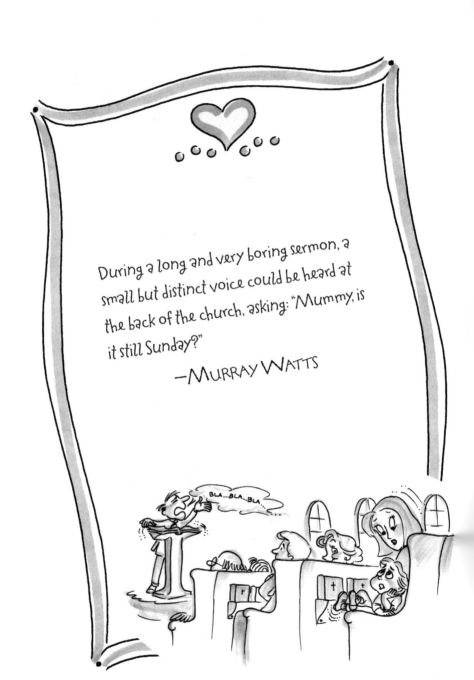

During a long and very boring sermon, a small but distinct voice could be heard at the back of the church, asking: "Mummy, is it still Sunday?"

—MURRAY WATTS

Who's Doing This?

Mary Hollingsworth

He was only five years old, but he had a big, booming voice with which he would, no doubt, become a preacher, or so his mother thought. He was the light of her life.

He was to be the ring bearer in the wedding, including tux, tails, and satin pillow. It was a dubious honor in his young opinion, but since he had to do it, he was totally in control of the situation.

Rehearsal went well, except that his mother thought he was walking a bit too fast down the aisle. At the wedding the next night his mother positioned herself about halfway down the bridal path on the seat next to the aisle so she could encourage her son to slow down.

As expected, when the procession started, his mother decided that Junior was moving too fast. Just as he got to her pew, she put her hand out and whispered, "Slow down, sweetheart."

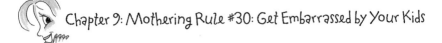

Insulted by the insinuation, Junior stopped midaisle, laid the satin pillow on the floor, backed off from his mother, put his little hands on his hips, and boomed, "Look here, woman! Who's doing this—me or you?"

The audience rippled with laughter, and his mother slid down into her pew, totally humiliated. Junior calmly straightened his little tux jacket, picked up the satin pillow, and solemnly marched to his appointed place at the front of the church. The rest of the wedding was, in comparison, uneventful.

Top 5 Ways to Spot a Mother on a Date

Becky Freeman

1. She immediately moves all salt, pepper, and sugar packets out of arm's reach.

2. She reaches in her purse, pulls out a baggy of Teddy Grahams, and offers them to her husband as a pre-dinner appetizer.

3. She gives her order to the waiter in baby talk. "Is the pasta that twisty around and around kind, or the itty-bitty baby snail shell kind? Because the twisty around and around kind tastes really yucky."

4. She stands up and tucks her husband's napkin under his chin. Then she returns to her seat, folds her napkin into the shape of a diaper, and lays it in her lap.

5. Before leaving the restaurant, she asks her husband, "Are you *sure* you don't need to go to the potty? It's a thirty-minute drive home now."

Foxes in the Henhouse

Fran Caffey Sandin

As I hurried to complete the Saturday morning chores, I waited with anticipation for our date! My husband had invited me to go out that evening—a special treat for any mother of three preschoolers. On this particular day, I felt especially in need of some pampering. That's when I spied the new jar of "oatmeal mask" on my bathroom vanity, touted to stimulate the skin and make it glow like a young girl's.

I turned the lid and sniffed at the mixture. *Hey, why not get gorgeous and get the vacuuming done at the same time,* I reasoned? I patted on an extra thick layer of the oatmeal formula, thinking it would take more than the ordinary dollop to beautify my stressed out and neglected skin. Then, while the children played, I shoved the droning machine back and forth. My face tingled as the oatmeal began to set, and I couldn't help feeling proud of my cleverness. I was accomplishing two important goals at the same time.

I had whirred my way into the last bedroom when, suddenly, I had the oddest feeling that someone was watching me. My back was to the bedroom door when I heard a man clear his throat. I clicked off the vacuum in time to hear his quick and desperate apology.

"Ma'am, excuse me, Ma'am. I didn't want to scare you, but your son invited me in, and I wanted to show you our new line of carpet sweepers."

By then my museum-like expression had set—frozen in time. I couldn't scream, smile, or even say a word. In slow motion, I turned around to face the man, my raccoon eyes peering out of the bumpy plastered mask.

The poor guy grew more startled with each of his goose-steps backwards. "Oh, oh, no, no," his eyes widened as he stuttered, "I-I, think I've made a mistake!" Then he whirled around and headed for the door, dragging his sweeper behind him. Safely outside, he broke into a run and is probably still running today, wondering, *Who was that masked woman?*

As I removed the mask, I noticed that my face was warm and glowing, but I wasn't sure if that was the result of anger, embarrassment, or the wonder-working oatmeal. Then I walked down the hall to have a heart-to-heart talk with our five-year-old. The little guy seemed genuinely oblivious to any wrongdoing.

"Steve," I asked, struggling to control my voice. "How did that man get into our house?"

"He rang the bell and you were busy," Steve replied innocently. "I was helping you, Mommy."

"Son, I realize you were trying to help," I squeaked out in the kindest voice I could muster, "but we don't want strangers walking into our house. Never invite anyone in unless Mommy or Daddy give their permission."

As a mother, I often struggled to maintain my sanity. Our youngsters were active and bright for which I was thankful; but I often felt inadequate for the task. How could I encourage their innocent trust and still teach my kids to be cautious?

Never invite anyone in unless Mommy or Daddy give their permission.

"Lord," I prayed, "help me to teach my little chicks to be wise to any foxes that sneak into their lives. But keep them innocent as lambs in Your presence." It wasn't long before a "fox" of a different sort entered our home leaving me unabashedly bewildered.

On the occasion of our ten-year-old daughter's birthday, she received a voluptuous teen-aged doll decked out like a Las Vegas showgirl. I didn't want to hurt the feelings of the child who gave the gift, so I kept quiet while the little girls "ooohed and aaahed."

After the party, my daughter Angie turned to me and asked sincerely, "Mother, you don't like the doll, do you?"

At that point, I didn't know what to do or say, so I flashed a quick silent prayer. *Dear Lord, please give me the wisdom. Help me be imaginative rather than destructive. This is one of those delicate situations, and I don't want to blow it.*

"Angie," I said brightly, "bring your doll into the bedroom and let's talk about it." Like two teenagers at a slumber party, we flopped on her bed and propped the doll up on a pillow.

Then I asked casually, "Honey, does anything bother you about this doll?"

She thought for a minute and said, "Well, her outfit is kind of, you know, it just doesn't seem like something I'd want to wear."

"I know what you mean," I sighed. "Kind of skimpy, isn't it? Oh, Angie, there is nothing wrong with having pretty hair or a good figure, but I want you to know those aren't the most important things. A person's character is so much more important. And what we wear says something to others about what's inside of us—don't you think?"

Angie nodded enthusiastically as I continued. "You've been wanting to learn how to use the sewing machine, and I think this is the perfect time. Let's go to the store, pick out some patterns and material, and whip up some beautiful new clothes for this little Miss Priss. What do you say?"

In the days and weeks that followed, my daughter and I spent hours working on the tiny garments. I had to get bifocals, and at times, I wanted to pull my hair out, but Angie was so proud of our designing efforts. While vacationing in historic Williamsburg, we even found a perfectly charming Southern Belle dress to add to the doll's now lavish wardrobe.

Some years later, I was surprised when Angie decided to put her beloved doll in a garage sale. Together, we went through a drawer full of carefully folded doll clothes that we had sewn together. It touched my heart to discover that she had so carefully preserved this symbol of our mother-daughter bonding and the happy hours of informal creativity we shared. "Oh, Father," I whispered, "thank You for those sweet memories."

Today my children are grown, and I look back with gratitude. During all my years of mothering, I learned one thing for sure. Our God has creative answers for all our mothering dilemmas. Funny. As I think back on those early days, I realize it was often the awkward situations that provided the best opportunities for teaching my children. From the vacuum salesman incident, my son learned to check with me before letting strangers into our home (especially when Mommy is wearing breakfast cereal on her face). And from a barely clad plastic doll, my daughter learned that part of being a beautiful girl means dressing creatively, fashionably, and modestly.

When we mothers ask Him, God is extraordinarily faithful to help us handle all life's little foxes—be they man or molded plastic—that creep into the henhouse.

Life with Mr. Comedy (a.k.a. "Dad")

A father is a banker provided by nature.

—FRENCH PROVERB

Superdad's Holiday Adventure

Phil Callaway

I learned a valuable lesson this week: If evolution were true, mothers would have three hands and an extra set of eyes in the back of their heads.

Last Friday, I was sitting at work, leaning back in my chair, counting the minutes until holidays began. Ah, it would be wonderful! Suddenly my chair back gave way and I hit my head on an old-fashioned radiator that sits in my office just waiting for this to happen.

Although we wouldn't be going far on this vacation (my wife was in the final stages of pregnancy and in a sour mood whenever I mentioned the drive to Alaska), I would finally be able to spend some quantity time with my two preschoolers. I would take them swimming, shopping, to the zoo, to the lake. They would sit and watch me as I worked on the car and cut the grass. They would

help me weed the garden. I would even pay them in quarters for their efforts. Ah, vacation! There's nothing quite like it. My lucky wife spent seven days a week at home with these little darlings as I slaved away near this radiator. Finally, it was my turn to relax.

Things started out pretty well. On our first evening together, I took the kids out for ice cream and they managed to get some in their mouths. But when we arrived home, Ramona informed me that it might be a good idea for us to go to the hospital—RIGHT THIS VERY MINUTE!

I remained perfectly calm. After all, this was not the first time we had gone through this ordeal.

"It's okay, it's okay," I assured her, "I'll be fine."

"Breathe deeply," she said. "Like they taught us in prenatal class."

After seven hours—which rank right up there with barefoot ice fishing—Jeffery was born. Although I applauded my wife and the miracle of birth, as I drove to pick up our other two angels from their grandparents' house, I wondered again if there wasn't a better way of reproducing. "Certain types of worms merely separate," I said to no one in particular.

> My lucky wife spent seven days a week at home with these little darlings. Finally, it was my turn to relax.

That night there was cause for celebration. After the angels were in bed, a friend dropped by to commemorate with me the birth of our third-born. 7-Up, peanuts, and a mediocre movie were the order of the evening, but by the time I went to bed I was thinking, *It's a good thing I'm on holidays. I shall need a little rest.*

As I dozed off, visions of summer sun danced through my head. Visions of that trip to the zoo. That boat-ride on the lake.

Visions of sipping Coke beneath the maple tree as the children played quietly around my feet.

Suddenly, there he was—pouncing on me.

"Hey Dad, time to get up."

"Whaaat? Where are we? Who are we? Who are *you?* What time is it?"

I groped for the clock. It was 7 A.M. Time for breakfast. After four hours of sleep. I would make the best of it. A meal with the kids. Time to get to know each other. Rachael smiled at me past three teeth. She was so sweet. I pinched her dimple gently. Her pink bib was so clean. Unlike her brother's. Rachael continued to smile at me as she deposited her bowl of soggy Cheerios on the floor. I smiled back. Stephen promptly dropped his piece of bread on the floor, jam side down. "But…Daddy," was all he said.

"That's okay."

Then he spilled his milk.

"But…Daddy."

By this time I thought we could all use a little fresh air, so off we went—grocery shopping. Now, I must confess that in years past I have been highly critical of supermarket mothers. Especially those with more than one child dangling from their shopping cart squeezing bruises into the peaches. Especially those who have had enough of the screaming and "accidentally" swap carts with other unsuspecting shoppers.

MOTHER: "Have you noticed that flour is $4.99?"

OTHER MOTHER: "I will pay you $499,000 to take my child till Wednesday!"

By the time we reached the checkout counter, I was looking—and feeling—just like one of them.

"What's that hanging from your cart, Mr. Callaway?"

"Oh, that's my eldest child."

"No, no. The red sticky stuff."

On the way home, Rachael remembered that she didn't appreciate being strapped into a car seat. Without a good set of ear plugs a trip to the zoo would be impossible. By nightfall I was exhausted, and I hadn't even done the dishes. Or swept the floor. Or cleaned the house. Or planned breakfast.

The next day dawned early. Again. *Why don't kids just sleep half the morning?* I thought. *I used to when I was in high school.* After another adventuresome breakfast, I put on a children's video and instructed the kids to watch quietly while Daddy rested on the living room floor. It was not a good idea. Fathers in that position should keep their eyes open. Mine were closed. Just as I began to doze off, Rachael brought her soggy diaper to rest on daddy's head.

Nightfall brought with it the promise of much-needed sleep. But it was not to be. Rachael wouldn't go to sleep. Daddy couldn't find her pacifier. And he was being punished.

I looked everywhere. Twice. Finally I found it in the heat vent. When I brought it to her, she was fast asleep.

"What does Jesus look like?" asked Stephen. *This is not the time. Can't he see Daddy is tired? Questions like this are to be asked after church. Or after a good rest.* I lay down beside him. This was the time for questions at our house.

"When will Mommy come home?"

"Soon," I answered. "Just two more sleeps." Then I began to confess my sins to my three-year-old. "Before I came home for holidays, I thought Mommy's work was easy. But then I saw the mess you two make, and how many diapers need changed.

Would you like to make the beds, wash the clothes, make meals, clean the house, change diapers?"

He screwed up his little nose.

"I'm thankful for Mommy," I continued. "I had no idea how hard she works."

He nodded. "She loves Jesus."

"Let's thank Him for her." I prayed out loud asking God's forgiveness for taking my wife for granted, and thanking Him for her hard work. Her unselfish love. Her joyful spirit.

When I looked over at Stephen, he was sound asleep.

And now it was my turn.

On my way to the bedroom I took one last look into Rachael's room. She was standing up in her crib smiling at me past three teeth. And looking for her pacifier.

You Rile the Kids Up, You Put 'Em to Bed!

Joey O'Connor

Who says guys don't know how to put the kids to bed? It's high time someone put this dastardly dad discrimination to rest. For years, guys have had to prove that they are both competent and capable at getting their kids to bed. I mean, how hard is it to get kids dressed, brushed, pottied, prayed, and tucked into bed?

Yes, every guy knows that his wife can zip through this necessary nightly ritual in less than ten minutes, but what's the big hurry? Guys know that their wives want to get the kids to bed early not because the kids need their rest, but because Mom needs hers—and besides, she wants to watch her favorite sitcom. Why make putting the kids to bed such a hurry-up-and-get-to-sleep system? Why make it so predictable? So routine? So one-dimensional? So boring.

Kids need to expand their horizons. They need their minds and bodies to be shaken and invigorated from that Jell-O-induced state caused by too much TV and Sega. They need to push the limits. Break the envelope. Maybe even break (moms will love this) the sound barrier. Kids need to go to extremes, and that's why God made dads.

Let's take a vote: Ask your kids who they'd prefer putting them to bed, Mom or Dad? Hands down, Dad wins. Kids love it when Dad puts them to bed because that means they'll get to stay up *at least* forty-five minutes longer.

Start with "peeyamas." Once he gets the kids into their bedrooms, the first major challenge the dad faces is *finding* his kids' peeyamas. For all he knows, the peeyamas could be in a drawer, a closet, a Barney suitcase, a wastebasket, or a hamper, or (most likely) under the bed. How is he supposed to know where his kids put their peeyamas? Once the peeyamas are located, the dad enters his first major battle of the evening when he squares off with his three-year-old daughter who insists on choosing which pair of peeyamas she wants to wear.

"Honey, wear the Tinkerbell jammies."

"No, I wanna wear Winnie Pooh."

"Aw c'mon, just wear the Tinkerbell jammies. They look so cute on you."

"I hate Tinkerbell!"

"We don't say that word in this house. Winnie Pooh never says that word."

"Okay, but do I have to wear the Tinkerbells?"

Sad, pleading, puppy eyes.

"I guess not—you can wear the Winnie Poohs."

Even though her head doesn't fit through the opening for the right arm, the little DWARF (Daddy Wrapped Around Right Finger) insists she can put on the Winnie Pooh jammies just fine on her own. Winnie Pooh ends up backward and inside out, but she declares, "I meant to do that."

Knowing better than to mess with a willful woman, the dad sits back on his haunches and waits. Having already lost two battles, the dad now needs to compensate by launching a Tickle Monster counteroffensive. Seeing his daughter in her jammies makes it completely impossible not to tickle her. The dad was created for this purpose.

> Kids know that by sitting on the potty they can eke more time out of going to bed.

As she squeals in high-pitched laughter, his older son tears into the bedroom, wearing Photon Destroyer peeyamas and screaming, "DEATH TO THE ALIEN SLIME SUCKERS," whereby he proceeds to knee-drop dear old Dad to the floor. The dad plays dead and allows his kids to pound on him for 7.8 seconds. Like a phoenix rising from the ashes, the dad yells in a thundering voice, "BLANKET RAID!" His kids scream loud enough to break the neighbors' windows, and his wife, who happens to be watching her favorite sitcom downstairs, shakes her head and tells herself not to get up.

Quick as a flash, Dad grabs the covers off his daughter's bed and, in one fell swoop, covers both kids who are now kicking and screaming like cats in a bag. Inevitably, both kids konk heads and Winnie Pooh begins crying.

"Okay," the Instigator asserts with a voice of authority and control, "settle down now."

Time to brush teeth.

Younger kids hate, oops, dislike using minty toothpaste because most dentist-recommended toothpaste feels hotter than Arizona asphalt in the middle of August. "It's too spicy," the kids cry as bubbly green foam drools down their faces.

Dads have a quick remedy for toothpaste burn victims. *Entertain them.* Putting a healthy dab on a toothbrush, the dad will work up a big glob of gooey foam and proceed to make toothpaste foam bubbles larger than his face. Not all dads aspire to such heights. Other variations on a theme include: Crazy Man Foaming at the Mouth, Foam on the Mirror, Foam Spit Tricks, and Foam Grenade.

Potty time.

During the potty portion of the bedtime routine, if Mom's in charge, the kids always have to go Number 1. If Dad's in charge, the kids always have to go Number 2.

Always.

From a physiological point of view, this is because twenty minutes of jumping on the bed, wrestling, and tickling produce enough activity to get the lower intestine moving and grooving.

From a psychological point of view, kids know that by sitting on the potty they can eke more time out of going to bed. By claiming to have to go Number 2, even giving the slightest mention of Number 2, they buy time because there's no way the dad is going to take any chances.

"You just sit there, honey, and take all the time you need. Wanna book?"

Now for prayer time.

Prayer time is a major spiritual event in our home. One time when I was saying prayers with Ellie, our four-year-old, I felt a

distinct little swipe across my forehead. I opened my eyes and looked at Ellie, who had a sneaky smile across her face.

"Ellie, what did you just do? Why'd you touch my forehead?"

"I wiped my goop."

That nostril deposit incited a furious tickling match and delayed prayer time another few minutes, which led to another series of distractions.

Distractions are what make it difficult for dads during prayer time. They're not used to fielding so many difficult questions. What is a dad really supposed to say when his kids ask how God turns the rain on or what Jonah looked like after he spent three days in the belly of a whale or why Noah allowed cockroaches and mosquitoes on the ark? Dads have a tough time answering such theological questions.

"Well, son, cockroaches play a very important role in making God laugh. You know how your mother and sisters jump up on the chairs and start screaming whenever they see an itty-bitty cockroach. God thinks that's funny and that's why He created cockroaches. They're also the only ones who'll eat your mother's cooking, but that's just between us men."

By the time the fifth glass of water has been drunk and 473 monsters have been killed under the bed, in the closet, and outside the window, and the eleventh "Just one more question—" has been answered, it is an hour and forty-five minutes later, but the kids are exhausted and go right to sleep. The sitcom is long over and the dad's wife is fast asleep.

See, that wasn't so bad.

Piece of cake.

Thar She Blows

Dave Meurer

Waking up next to a pregnant woman is like waking up next to a motion-detecting bomb. You really, *really* can't afford one false move.

Have you ever seen one of those movies where the insane villain holds the damsel-in-distress hostage by strapping an explosive device to her body? If she so much as twitches—KABOOM!

That's where the brave hero comes in and, risking his own life, rescues her.

With a pregnancy, the husband gets to play the role of *both* the insane villain and the brave hero. The plot is simple: he got her into this mess, and he had better rescue her.

When my wife, Dale, was pregnant for the first time, she woke up horribly nauseous one morning. She desperately wanted

a saltine cracker, but I did not know this because she was so queasy she could only manage to moan, "Crerr."

Well, "crerr" is not a word I recognized.

"What?" I asked.

"Crerr!" she whispered, frozen in place, with a desperate look on her brow.

"Do you want me to get you something?" I asked.

"Crerr," she nodded, ever so slightly.

"Bacon and eggs OK?"

"KABOOM!" went the hostage.

She later explained—rather testily—that "crerr" means, "I want you to get me a cracker and some warm tea IMMEDI-ATELY before I get violently ill, but you need to ease out of bed very s-l-o-w-l-y so you don't jostle me."

Regrettably, there is an inherent contradiction in the directive to do something both "immediately" and "slowly." So we had a few more KABOOMS until I at least "sort of" mastered the technique, which was (1) levitate out of bed without so much as brushing against a sheet molecule; (2) make a cup of mild tea, with just three granules of sugar to take out the bitterness; and (3) have both the tea and the cracker ready for her the split second she wakes up.

As you can imagine, these were tense mornings.

Besides, I think it is a pretty big deal for the hero to rescue the damsel *once*—but EVERY SINGLE DAY for three solid months?

Our good friends Tim and Pam also shared the pregnancy experience. Pam, too, was stricken with morning sickness—only it was more like "morning, afternoon, and evening sickness."

"At first I was right by her side every time she ran for the bath-

room," Tim told me. "I would get her a glass of water and a washcloth and pat her back and practically be in tears, I felt so bad for her."

But as time wore on, he found himself just calling out, "You doing OK in there?"

Toward the end, this devolved into Tim remarking, "Hey, try not to spill my nachos!" as Pam bolted from the bed and dove for the porcelain target.

Tim would just continue watching TV or reading his book.

Now, it isn't that guys are insensitive Neanderthals, it's just that the routine starts to get a little old after awhile. Besides, it isn't like we can make our wives feel better anyway. I mean, if we *could* we certainly *would,* but even with the tea and crackers and all our best efforts, the odds are that Old Faithful is going to blow sky-high anyway. So we guys tend to get a little fatalistic.

Pregnancy does REALLY weird things to a woman.

But even if I survived the daily morning disarmament drill, I was by no means home free. Pregnancy does REALLY weird things to a woman, including, in Dale's case, creating an insatiable need for stir-fried cabbage at nine o'clock at night. Nothing else would do. And she wanted it NOW!

So I would speed to the store to buy enough cabbage to feed the entire convention of vegetarians. But the next night, cabbage was out and zucchini was in. Menu planning was impossible. The clock would strike nine, and only then would the mystery craving be revealed—and it was almost always some offbeat substance

that we did not have readily available in the cupboard, such as steamed paprika on rye.

I have never heard an adequate explanation for the bizarre food desires of pregnant women. Not that I doubt for a moment that these wild desires are real. On the contrary, they are a staple of pregnant-woman lore through the centuries. But WHY?

Aside from the obvious fact that her body is seeking certain nutrients to keep the developing baby healthy, I have a hunch that this is yet another one of those "God things"—like making sure our babies require diaper assistance when He could have just as easily let them take in carbon dioxide and give off oxygen like your basic Boston fern.

Pregnant animals don't ask for special diets. Mrs. Lion doesn't say to Mr. Lion, "Yuck! Keep that dead wildebeest away from me and get me a peach yogurt!"

No, animals just keep eating the same old thing they've always eaten.

But women turn into moody, weepy, goofy, sleepy, irritable insomniacs with food allergies—sometimes all in the space of five minutes. The net result is that guys are given the opportunity to be *more* supportive, *more* understanding, *more* patient, *more* protective, and *more* loving than ever before. Which, of course, is precisely what God wants from us anyway, so it only increases my suspicion that this state of affairs is not simply a coincidence.

Further bolstering my "God-thing" theory is the fact that infants *also* tend to be moody, weepy, goofy, sleepy, irritable insomniacs with food allergies! So it looks very much like God has arranged pregnancy as a sort of parenthood "boot camp," except that the person who eventually yells at you at four o'clock

in the morning at the top of his lungs is much shorter than a typical drill sergeant, plus he has a wet diaper.

The truly amazing thing about pregnancy is that, even with all its inherent dangers and difficulties, most men survive it.

Chapter 11

Cooking Up Comedy

I serve leftovers the easy way. I never clear the table.

—MARTHA BOLTON

A Baking Recipe for Mothers

Becky Freeman

1. Preheat the oven. Check to be sure there are no rubber balls or plastic soldiers lurking on the racks.

2. Remove blocks and toy cars from table. Grease pan. Crack nuts.

3. Measure two cups flour. Remove Johnny's hands from the flour. Wash flour off him. Re-measure flour.

4. Crack more nuts to replace those that Johnny ate. Put flour, baking powder, and salt in sifter. Get dust pan and brush up pieces of bowl that Johnny knocked on the floor. Get another bowl.

5. Answer the doorbell. Return to kitchen. Remove Johnny's hands from the bowl again. Wash Johnny. Answer the phone. Return to kitchen.

6. Remove 1/2-inch salt from the greased pan. Look for Johnny. Grease another pan. Answer phone. Return to kitchen and find Johnny.

7. Take up greased pan and remove layer of nut shells in it. Head for Johnny who runs, knocking the bowl off the table.

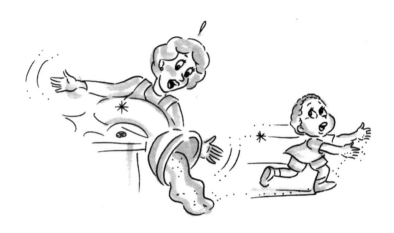

A Smashing Success in the Kitchen

Karen Scalf Linamen

I'll never forget the week my sister Renee Berge flew to Dallas for a visit. The days were filled with a flurry of warm-fuzzy, memory-making Kodak moments. Renee and I not only caught up on the details of each other's lives, we enjoyed watching our young kids—her sons Conner, Hunter, and Isaac, and my daughters Kaitlyn and Kacie—rediscover the joys of cousinhood after nearly a year apart.

I collected lots of warm family memories from that week.

For instance, there was the bonding that took place between Renee and me as we honed our teamwork, working side by side to scrub Hunter's crayoned artwork from the stairwell walls before Larry got home from work. To this day he doesn't realize that there's no paint on half the stairwell wall. What he *thinks* is paint is actually the drywall. We were lucky it was only a shade

away from the color the paint used to be before it all got scrubbed off with cleanser.

Another warm family memory is the time Renee and I were in the kitchen making some sort of dessert that called for crushed vanilla wafers. I was beginning to dig around for my rolling pin when Renee grabbed the box of cookies and my car keys and headed out the front door. "Don't worry—," she hollered behind her, "I'll take care of it."

The kids, sensing adventure, followed her onto the porch.

She returned several minutes later and handed me the cookies. They were beautifully crushed, although the box didn't look so hot.

"What'd you do?" I asked.

"I wedged the box behind the right front tire of your van and then popped the engine into reverse."

"YOU RAN OVER THE COOKIES?"

She glanced at the recipe before heading toward the refrigerator for the next ingredient on the list. I got there first. "You did great with the cookies," I said with admiration, "but maybe you should let me handle the eggs."

My On-and-Off Struggle with Manuals

Marti Attoun

When Mom needed to know how to light the pilot on our old wall furnace, she consulted its instructions, which were printed on a thin leaflet stabbed on a nail in the utility room closet.

Today, we need the whole closet, not just the nail, to store all the bloated leaflets and manuals that accompany machines found in the average house. Who says we aren't a nation of readers? Shucks. Before you can use a new electric skillet, you're supposed to read its 12-page manual. I'm sure there's a lawyer behind all this.

Like most people, we have a library of this literature that accompanies our time-saving machines. We can't save enough time, though, to read it.

So we fiddle and poke around and try to operate the equipment without reading the instructions. Then we find any helpful kid over age 3 because they're all born techies.

The other day, for example, I broke down and bought a simple new answering machine. The hardest part of the operation should have been pruning the Ozarks from my accent so I wouldn't sound like Aunt Birdie's Biskit Barn should some important editor call.

I killed 10 minutes trying to get the already-recorded message from the strange man out of the machine. He sounded pleasant, a nice guy to have around the house, but I knew good and well that my mother would never talk to him. That meant I could miss an important call from her—such as an invitation to run over and retrieve that homemade pumpkin pie cooling on her cabinet.

Finally, I offered my 13-year-old a buck to teach me how to record a message on the machine.

He smirked. "Make it $10 and I'll set the clock for you, too," he said.

It took him under three seconds, which isn't a bad hourly wage.

Everything with a cord in our house has a manual, but the fattest manuals came boxed with the microwave. One is for "basic" microwaving, and the sequel is for "advanced."

Limp from hunger one night, I begged the little techie to help me defrost a T-bone.

"If you'll help me put the on-time switch in the five-minute position," I told him, "I think I can handle it from there." I'd been puzzling over the advanced manual so long that I could have cooked the steak on a stick over a campfire.

"You're reading the manual for the motion sensor light," my son pointed out.

You've read one manual you've read them all: thin plot, excess verbiage. They're all a real turnoff...if you can just find the switch.

Chapter 12

Family Frivolity

In the Clutches of Summer
Marti Attoun

As we neared Florida and some relatives that my 11-year-old son had never met, he mumbled the question that he'd been mulling for many miles.

"I wonder if they're huggers?"

I could have lied and said that, after traveling 1,200 miles, we'd probably all greet each other by saluting. Worse, I could have told the truth that someday he, too, would convert from huggee to hugger. I didn't want him to gag, though.

"Yes, it's possible that you'll be hugged," I warned. "Just hold your breath and think about something good, like summer."

Every family harbors some dyed-in-the-wool huggers who mark arrivals and departures with enthusiastic squeezes. The grownups never seem to notice or be bothered; the kids always do.

My childhood summers were framed by the arms of the

huggers, who visited from western Kansas each year. As soon as Mom announced that Uncle Jim and Aunt Nadine were on the horizon, my sisters and I would giggle and plot our strategy as we camped on the divan. It was a tan three-piece sectional, which Mom frequently divided and shuffled around the room. We strategically occupied one slice.

"I'm going first to get it over with," my sister Rose would whisper.

"Maybe they'll be talking up a blue streak with Mom and won't notice us," Winnie would say.

My sisters and I would giggle and plot our strategy as we camped on the divan.

Mom knew exactly what we were up to. "Now, girls, be nice," she'd say. "You haven't seen Uncle Jim and Aunt Nadine since last summer."

Of course, we would be nice. But how could one tiny woman, no bigger than a blue jay, have arms that stretched longer than our living room?"

The minute Mom heard their car tires crunch the gravel driveway, she was out the door. Uncle Jim's laughter floated across the front yard and spilled onto the porch and into the house.

And there they stood. Aunt Nadine peeled her pocketbook off her arm and set it on the TV. The two of them beamed at us, arms wide open and empty.

Uncle Jim scooped up Rose. Then, "Come here, you little sweetie pie," Aunt Nadine squealed at me.

There's no escaping, I told myself. It's the spinach of summer. Slurp it down, then you're finished until the next visit. I inched off the divan.

Aunt Nadine swooped me into her arms, which smelled like lemon bath powder. "I'd like to squeeze the stuffin' out of you, you little dickens," she said between squeezing. "Just look how big you've grown."

I couldn't look. I was locked against her bosom, suddenly as vast as western Kansas, waiting for her to stop patting my back so I could exhale. After forever, she released me, and I swapped places with Rose.

We three huggees giggled after this ritual. Finally, summer had officially arrived.

The Roosters in Our Family Tree

Gracie Malone

May I kiss him?" our three-year-old grandson, Montana, asked as I started to place newborn Myles back in his cradle. I sat in the rocking chair, opened up the blanket, and watched as Montana kissed his little brother on the cheek. "Can I give him a hug?" he asked. When I nodded "yes," Montana put his arms around Myles's tiny shoulders and gently squeezed. "Let me tell him a secret." I cradled Myles in my arms while Montana leaned close to the baby's ear and whispered a secret message—something that no other person would ever know.

Throughout the day, at the most unexpected times, while watching *Toy Story* or playing with Mr. Potato Head™, Montana's thoughts would turn toward Myles and he'd jump up and ask, "May I kiss him? Give him a hug? Tell him a secret?" As I watched this tender scene unfold again and again, I thought about the special bond that exists between brothers—a bond that begins at birth, a bond so tight that even mothers and grandmothers are left wondering what the secret could possibly be.

As the mother of three sons, this wasn't the first time I'd seen the unique brotherhood that exists between guys born into the same family. Our oldest son, Matt, was two and a half when we brought his little brother, Mike, home from the hospital and gently laid him in the antique cradle that had rocked six generations of family members. One morning soon afterward, I heard a muffled voice coming from the baby's room. When I ran to check it out, there was Matt stretched out beside his brother, Mike's tiny fingers curled around Matt's slightly bigger ones. When I lifted him out of the cradle and explained why a big boy shouldn't climb into bed with such a tiny baby, Matt offered this simple excuse: "But, I wanted to tell him a story."

As they grew older, the bond between Matt and Mike grew stronger and secrets multiplied. I didn't find out the truth about some of their antics until after they were grown.

One summer we visited our friends in North Carolina—Gail, Virgil, and their three sons, Brian, Roger, and Daniel. On Friday night we put five little boys to bed early, and played bridge until the wee hours of the morning. Before we headed for the roost, I came up with a brilliant idea. "Let's put the cereal and the bowls on the table, and leave some milk in a small pitcher in the fridge. When the kids get up, they can eat breakfast and watch cartoons, while we sleep in."

The next morning when Gail stumbled into the kitchen and headed for the coffee pot, she found brightly colored cereal

plastered all over the front of the refrigerator. Little trails of milk ran down the porcelain and dripped onto the floor. All experiments contain an element of risk, but this was appalling.

We finally learned that our precious sons had used their spoons as catapults, launching round after round of colorful ammunition at the white target. But to this day, it's still a mystery who came up with the idea or who did it first. With every question we asked, the ties that bind one brother to another grew tighter than the knots in their tennis shoe laces.

Throughout his grade school days and into the junior high years, Mike coveted Matt's "big brother" status with its privileges (and responsibilities). So about the time our number two son entered preadolescence, he started asking for a little brother. Needless to say, he received a somewhat-less-than-receptive response from me. So he went over my head and petitioned the one person he knew for certain would grant his wish—God. When I heard his prayers, I thought, I'd better feather my nest for a new baby chick.

Sure enough, Jason was born when Mike was twelve. That he was born on January first proved symbolic—new beginnings and a wide range of new experiences awaited us.

Before we brought him home from the hospital, my mother realized we needed help and decided to come for a visit. The first night, Jason was a toy. We played with him until bedtime, then slipped a cute little gown over his head, pulled the drawstring tight, placed him in the antique cradle, and settled down for a long winter's nap. At two o'clock in the morning, that cuddly little baby went off like a smoke alarm, and all five of us—Joe, Matt, Mike, Mother, and I—collided in the hallway, looking for the nearest exit.

From that night on, Jason's big brothers considered him their own personal charge. In addition to seeing that his basic needs were met, they made sure he enjoyed the coolest and best of life's experiences—a drop of lemon juice on his pacifier, a sip of pop, a taste of pizza, edited versions of "Monty Python." By the time he was three, Jason was a teen in a preschooler's body—more comfortable with a football than a stuffed toy, more in tune with "rock and roll" than lullabies, and most comfortable in a tiny pair of jeans and one of his kid-sized college T-shirts. He'd been biking, water skiing, camping, and motorcycling. He accompanied his brothers to football games, friends' houses, and the convenience store parking lot. (Matt finally confessed that Jason attracted girls like a magnet. "Why, he gets more attention than my Irish setter!")

At two o'clock in the morning, that cuddly little baby went off like a smoke alarm.

At home, Jason would likely be clutching a tattered and faded blue blanket as he perched on Mike's back to watch TV or sat on the hood of Matt's sports car cheering the teens shooting hoops in our driveway. And he was always giggling over something whispered into his ear.

By the time Matt and Mike went away to college, they were confident that Jason was thoroughly prepared for kindergarten—after all, they had already taught him several of the basic laws of science and physics. I came home from the grocery store one day and found Matt holding Jason upside down over the banister on the second floor level. Mike stood on the first floor with his arms extended to catch him in case Matt's hands slipped. "We're just teaching him about the laws of gravity," they explained as I

fussed and sputtered. They taught him about aerodynamics by sending him running as fast as he could go through the living room dodging flying pillows. They taught him physics by spinning him around and around in circles, then watching him fall in a crumpled heap. They helped him discover the beauty of God's creation by having him look up toward heaven until his face was covered with light, fluffy snowflakes.

When Matt and Mike went away to school, Jason did quite well on his own, developing into a sensitive, strong, intelligent guy, with lots of close friends. And he kept in touch with his brothers regularly by phone. When Jason finished college, I wasn't surprised that Matt offered him a job. "Come to work for us, and I'll teach you all I know about how to run a business."

It seems to me that the sentiment Montana expressed toward Myles is still being passed down from brother to brother. Oh, I know they would gag to think about puckering up for a kiss, but I have seen them exchange a few awkward hugs. And they are still sharing secrets.

How good and pleasant it is when brothers live together in unity! (Psalm 133:1).

Guest of Honor

Martha Bolton

Not long ago, it became necessary to replace our old dining room set. It was beginning to sag in the middle (from years of holding up my biscuits, no doubt), and it bore numerous knife marks and scratches (from dinner guests who had opted for the easier task of cutting through it instead of my meatloaf).

In its place we bought a new French provincial dining table along with six chairs, two leaves, and a shine you could tan by. It was beautiful. Day after day, week after week, I'd walk past it admiringly. My husband would comment on how nice it looked. My children were even impressed.

Then, the inevitable came. One day, my eldest son asked if we were ever planning to eat off it or were we merely saving it for a souvenir.

He had a point.

I don't know why it is, but too often we tend to save our best and newest things for company.

My good china is in my buffet collecting dust while the family and I eat off designer Dixieware.

My fine crystal is in boxes shoved in a cupboard while we drink out of souvenir Slurpee cups from 7-Eleven.

I even have brand-new bedsheets that I've been saving for guests. Meanwhile, my husband and I get the ones that only fit when I roll up our mattress like a croissant.

But my son's comment that day reminded me it doesn't have to be like that. After all, what dinner guests could be more important to me than my own family.

So, right then and there, I determined things were going to be different. I was going to treat my family to a very special "company" type meal (you know, where you use forks).

This time, when my son walked by the table, he looked at his crystal-clear reflection in the china, which I had meticulously placed around the table, and naturally inquired, "How does my hair look?"

Then he went on to ask, "Someone special coming for dinner tonight, Mom?"

I nodded.

"You're looking at him."

Chapter
13

Those Amusing
Adolescents

When God created Adam and Eve, you'll notice he skipped the teenage years.

—MARTHA BOLTON

A Mother's Instructions to Her Teenage Driver

Nancy Chapman Monroe

Don't speed.
CALL ME.
Don't pass cars on curves.
In fact, *don't pass cars!*
Or trucks. Especially trucks. Those big ones.
CALL ME.
Pay attention to road signs.
Don't speed.
Obey all traffic signals.
CALL ME.
Don't pick up hitchhikers.
Even if you know them.
—even if it's your grandmother!
CALL ME.

Don't fiddle with the radio/tape deck/CD player while driving.
Maybe you shouldn't listen to music at all.
Don't run caution lights.
CALL ME.
Watch everything going on around you.
Don't take your eyes off the road!
Don't speed.
Don't forget to wear your seatbelt.
Make sure everybody wears a seatbelt.
CALL ME.
Drive slower in the rain.
Maybe you should pull over in the rain.
Don't sit on the side of the road too long!
Don't speed.
Use your turn signals properly.
CALL ME.

A Mother's Guide to Cool
Kathy Peel

1. If a teenager asks if your head got caught in a ceiling fan, it's time for a new hair style.

2. If you hear your teenager's friends refer to you using the term "Dork Massive," take the hint and update your wardrobe.

3. Never admit your favorite television program is *The Flying Nun.*

4. Never do your Doris Day impersonation in front of teenagers.

5. Never laugh with cottage cheese in your mouth.

6. If your teenager asks if all mothers wear support hose under their bathing suits, don't show up at their next pool party.

7. If you hear a song from your era on the radio, remember teenagers consider mime your best range.

8. Don't brag about the time you won the Miss Bell Aircraft Second Shift beauty contest.

9. Understand that teenagers couldn't care less about what happened when you were their age.

10. Never offer your teenager's friends liver, tuna casserole, or prune juice.

When I Lost the Need to Know

Lynn Assimacopoulos

I can nearly remember the exact moment several years ago when I began to lose credibility with my children. When they turned into teenagers, I started having difficulty functioning while they were in the same room. Once when we were on vacation and in a hotel room, I refused to try to set the digital clock. Of course my teenagers, never having seen this particular clock before, seemed to be able to work every button. The hotel drapes should have been fairly simple to manage, but I couldn't even get those opened. Instead I almost poked my eye out on some new-fangled plastic rod.

"Just pull that plastic rod, Mom. What's the matter?" asked one of my teenagers. "Don't you know how to open curtains?"

"I used to," I answered.

Why is it that a teenage boy who never owned a microwave can show you how it works 10 seconds after it's out of the box. He can learn a computer so fast it sends your brain spinning! He can hook up all kinds of wires to stereos, lighting systems, guitars and amplifiers without instructions. But ask him to run the weed-eater and he doesn't know how!

I ask myself that if teenage boys are so good at some things then why can't they?

Aim and hit the wastebasket.

Put their clothes in the closet on hangers.

Study without the TV and stereo on.

Use a plate for potato chips and pretzels.

Turn OFF a light switch.

Mow the lawn or shovel the snow without 12 bathroom breaks.

Remember to put gas in the car.

Drink from a glass instead of the milk carton.

Go to the library more than 2 hours before a term paper is due.

Ask to play an *inexpensive* band instrument.

Turn on a lamp when reading in the dark.

Shave even if they only have 5 (long) hairs on their face.

Leave a note at least every third day as to their whereabouts when you have not seen them awake and upright recently.

Stop saving old candy and gum wrappers in their underwear drawers.

Write legibly.

I had five years of college! I am an educated person! Yet there was that point when my college age sons began to write term papers on psychology, philosophy and micro-organisms that read as if they were from another galaxy. I just didn't get it!

Maybe sometimes I look stupid wearing thick socks in my

dress shoes to stretch them out. So what! So I don't always pro-
nounce "parmesan" and "pasta" right. So what! Once, only once,
did I call the accelerator in the car the "footfeet" (or was it the
"footfeed"?). Even my 80-year-old mother couldn't believe I said
that. So what if I get confused trying to run the VCR. I can program it to record something 2, 3, or 4 weeks from now, but can't
seem to get it to run at this very moment.

I think that I am an intelligent person. I work. I run a household. I am very organized. I give professional presentations. I can
speak to co-workers in an articulate way.
People say I do a good job. I have friends.
So what has happened to me?

The truth is that we all know different
"stuff" at different times. It's like everything else that is based on the need to
know. A teenager needs to know about
wires and speakers to communicate with
his friends. He needs to know about com-

Why can a
teenage boy who
never owned a
microwave show
you how it works
right out of
the box.

puters in order to "surf the Net" like his peers. These things are
important to his present life. He will learn to turn off the lights
when *he* is paying the light bill, he will learn to plan, get information and write a good paper when *his* paycheck depends on it,
he will learn to have plenty of gas in the car when *he* is traveling
with his own teenagers.

Back when I was a teenager, it was not yet my time to need to
know all about computers and VCRs. (I am getting better at the
computer, however. I'm still not so sure about the VCR.) I developed the need to know how to run the VCR because I did not
want to miss seeing some of the things my grandchildren were
doing. At a former job I was actually forced to have a need to

know about using a computer when a secretary quit and all my information was on the computer. Somehow I had to get that information out of there! I have come to the conclusion that I will never live long enough to learn everything that even my own computer does. Computers will keep me busy the rest of my functional life. If I had not had that urgent need to know, I would not have the job I have now or be writing these thoughts now.

When we have that need to know, we will learn and we will pick and choose our "stuff" to know just like the teenager. And there will always be more "stuff" to know. Life is so full of interesting information that we indeed must choose. Then there is plenty of other "stuff" that I don't even want to begin to know. Like the stock market or politics. (Besides, I am still working on the VCR!)

There is one item on life's agenda that is NOT based on the need to know. And that is to know God and his love. We do not need complicated directions. We do not need a college degree. We actually don't even have to be organized or articulate. We can be in our homes or homeless, we can have skin of any color, we can be poor or rich, we can be happy or sad, we can be old or young. We can even be angry with God. We can accept God's love anytime, anyplace without waiting for a "need to know" urge.

Chapter 14

Kids Will Be Kids

A pastor was talking to a group of young children about being Christians and going to Heaven. At the end of his talk, he asked, "Where do you want to go?"

"Heaven!" they all piped up.

Again, the pastor asked, "And what do you have to be to get there?"

"Dead!" one boy yelled.

—STAN TOLER

Let There Be Light

Susan Duke

Do you think bears live in these woods?" asked six-year-old Tyler.

"Well, they just might," his grandfather answered.

"Have you ever seen one?" chimed four-year-old Rachel.

"No, but I may have heard one growl once," her grandfather humored her.

Tyler's deep brown eyes twinkled as he continued his query about the woodland creatures occupying the dense woods surrounding our log home.

Brenda, my stepdaughter, tucked the kids in bed for the night after a long day of catching grasshoppers in a jar, enjoying a hearty country supper, and taking bubble baths. Afterwards, she joined us in the living room, but soon noticed the bedroom light was on again.

She heaved a tired sigh as she trudged back down to turn the light off once more. She'd just returned and plopped on the sofa when the light clicked on again. We heard Tyler and Rachel chattering away.

"Let me see what I can do," I offered, sensing Brenda's exasperation.

Reaching their room, I turned out the light, sat on the edge of the bed, and asked, "Don't you know if your mom has to come in here one more time, you're going to really be in trouble?"

"But we don't want the light off!" whined Rachel.

"Do you sleep with it on at home?" I asked

"No."

"Then why do you want it on here?"

"'Cause we're scared," Tyler offered.

"Scared of what? You're safe here!"

"Well, do the bears ever come up to the house at night?" asked Tyler.

"Of course not! Your granddad was just kidding you! There are no bears out here! You never have to be afraid. Besides, Jesus lives in your heart, so even in the dark, there's a light shining there all the time." I kissed them goodnight and turned off the light.

Ten minutes passed when, once more, filtered light came shining down the hallway. I bounded toward the bedroom, disappointed they would take our words so lightly.

"What's the deal, kids?"

"Well…we know Jesus is in here," Tyler explained. "And we know he's not scared. But he also talks to you in your heart and he just said he'd rather sleep with the light on."

Relatively Perfect
Mark Lowry

The other day while eating lunch with my older brother, Mike, I came up with the idea to write a routine about what it must have been like to be one of Jesus' younger siblings. How would it have felt to have a perfect older brother? Mike pointed out that I shouldn't have any problems relating to that.

But think about it.

Imagine what it must have been like to be one of Jesus' brothers or sisters.

Life around Joseph and Mary's household must have been pretty hard with Jesus for an older brother.

For one thing, it's probably safe to say that Baby Jesus hardly ever cried. He knew that in whatsoever state he was, therewith to be content. He didn't throw tantrums or dump his oatmeal on his head. He was no doubt the perfect baby.

He surely didn't go through the "terrible twos." While other two-year-olds were acting like miniature battering rams in diapers, destroying everything in their path, Jesus was sitting quietly in his chair, trying to remember why he ever bothered to create such rowdy two-year-olds. He obeyed his parents, never stayed up past his bedtime, or screamed "Mine! Mine! Mine!" while playing with a neighbor's toy. He had to be a parent's dream.

As a matter of fact, Mary and Joseph probably had such an easy time raising Jesus that they later decided to have children of their own.

And that's where the trouble surely kicked in. As long as Mary stayed with just the immaculately conceived baby, childrearing was a breeze. But as soon as Joseph started fathering their offspring, there was trouble right there in Nazareth city.

Think what Jesus' brothers and sisters must have heard from their mother every day:

"Why don't you act like your older brother?"

"Jesus never talks back."

"Jesus never leaves his robe and sandals lying around the house."

"Jesus doesn't have to be reminded to do his homework."

It had to have been tough—so tough that I've been told Jesus' siblings weren't believers until after his resurrection. They had a hard time acknowledging that their older brother was the Creator of the universe.

My brother and I couldn't even agree which one of us was going to reign over the television remote.

That's because my brother, however perfect he seems to me, isn't Jesus, and was born with the same sinful nature as mine.

I may not have had Mary suggesting to me that I should be more like Jesus. But every once in a while, in much gentler tones than even a mother could utter, the Spirit of God has said, "Hey, Mark, cut it out!"

Letter from Camp

Richard W. Bimler and Robert D. Bimler

Dear Mom and Dad,

We are having a great time here at Lake Typhoid. Scoutmaster Webb is making us all write to our parents in case you saw the flood on TV and worried. We are okay. Only one of our tents and two sleeping bags got washed away. Luckily, none of us got drowned because we were all up on the mountain looking for Chad when it happened. Oh yes, please call Chad's mother and tell her he is okay. He can't write because of the cast. We never would have found him in the dark if it hadn't been for the lightning. Scoutmaster Webb got mad at Chad for going on a hike alone without telling anyone. Chad said he did tell him, but it was during the fire so he probably didn't hear him. Did you know that if you put gas on a fire, the gas can will blow up? The wet wood still didn't burn, but one of our tents did. Also some of our clothes. John is going to look weird until his hair grows back. We will be home on Saturday if Scoutmaster Webb gets the car fixed. It wasn't his fault about the wreck. The brakes worked okay when we left. Scoutmaster Webb said that with a car that old, you have to expect something to break down; that's probably why he can't get insurance on it. We think it's a neat car. He doesn't care if we get it dirty, and if it's hot, sometimes he lets us ride on the tailgate. It gets pretty hot with ten people in a car. He let us take turns riding in the trailer until the highway patrolman stopped and talked to us. Scoutmaster Webb is a neat guy. Don't worry. He's a good driver.

John is going to look weird until his hair grows back.

He is teaching Terry how to drive. But he only lets him drive on the mountain roads where there isn't any traffic. All we ever see up there are logging trucks. This morning all of the guys were diving off the rocks and swimming out in the lake. Scoutmaster Webb wouldn't let me because I can't swim and Chad was afraid he would sink because of his cast, so he let us take the canoe across the lake. It was great. You can see the trees under the water from the flood. Scoutmaster Webb isn't crabby like some scoutmasters. He didn't even get mad about the life jackets. He has to spend a lot of time working on the car so we are trying not to cause him any trouble. Guess what? We have all passed our first-aid merit badges. When Dave dove in the lake and cut this arm, we got to see how a tourniquet works. Also Wade and I threw up. Scoutmaster Webb said it probably was just food poisoning from the leftover chicken. I have to go now. We are going into town to mail our letters and buy bullets. Don't worry about anything. We are fine.

P.S. How long has it been since I had a tetanus shot?

15

Where There's Motherhood

Rev. Dan Yeary of the North Phoenix Baptist Church in Arizona recently quoted a five-year-old's version of John 3:16: "For God so loved the world that He gave His only begotten son, that whosoever believeth in Him should not perish, but have ever-laughing life."

—CAL AND ROSE SAMRA

Ha! Ha! LIFE te-he!

Laugh and Lollygag

Lindsey O'Connor

I grabbed my keys and headed out the door to pick up my children from school. I was thankful for a break in my difficult day. *I'll enjoy the drive,* I thought. But then I discovered that my car was so dead that the starter didn't even click, let alone turn over. One of my four "meddlers" had left a light on in the car overnight. I called a friend to help me jump it, but it still wouldn't start so she loaned me her car. No problem. I knew I could zip over and get the kids and zip right back. She asked me to drop off Teresa, her cleaning lady, at the bus stop on the way back. No problem.

I picked up my three school-aged children who crowded into the hot car along with Teresa and her baby. The car trouble had made me late to get my children, and Teresa asked me in broken English if we were going to be late for her bus. It was almost 90

degrees outside, and there were four children and two adults in a tiny car with no air conditioning and 260,000 miles of wear and tear. I could sense a problem heading my way.

As I was about to peak the hill of the freeway overpass, the car's get-up-and-go got up and went. I was stranded on an incline in the middle lane. Since the car wouldn't go forward, I had only one option—backwards. I made sure everyone had fastened their seatbelts and then eyed my goal: the gas station at the bottom of the hill behind me. I explained my plan and my passengers said, "You're going to do WHAT?" I assured them it would be "no problem" as long as everyone driving forward in the lane behind me got out of the way.

> Like a crazy woman, I made wild arm circles, sign language for "Everybody get out of the way!"

With sweaty palms and a racing heart, I rolled down my window and, like a crazy woman, made wild arm circles, sign language for "Everybody get out of the way!" Miraculously, they did until one car pulled up behind me while I was still coasting towards the station, forcing me to brake short of my goal. *What is she doing?…Oh, helping me.*

She offered me a quarter, and I called my friend to tell her the great news about her car. She said, "No problem. I'll borrow Kay's car and be right there." When she got to Kay's house, she was red-faced and breathing hard. Kay said, "Lois, did you run all the way here?"

"No," Lois gasped. "I rode my bike, but both the tires were flat."

We were certainly having our problems.

When Lois got within a block of us, she started honking the

horn in "here I am to save the day" fashion and, for some reason, that struck Teresa funny and she started to laugh (which was amazing considering she'd just missed her bus). Laughing knows no language barrier, and she got me tickled. One of the children said, "Why are you laughing? I don't see a thing funny about this!" Then Lois told us about the flat tires and that did it—we all roared!

Two broken cars and two flat bike tires, hot children, frustrated women, and a missed bus—we had definite reasons to lose our cool, but we didn't. While teetering between the "I'm going to be joyful" and "I'm gonna lose it!" options, we decided to jump on the joy side and see the humor in the situation. Laughter softened our tough afternoon and made a great memory for my kids. It also gave our friends in our small Bible study an opportunity—at my expense—for a good howl. Somehow they found great humor in picturing me (and, I might add, imitating me) waving like mad while I coasted backwards downhill with sweaty, squished, scared passengers. But three cheers for laughter! It certainly helps lighten our load!

When All Else Fails, Laugh

Charlene Ann Baumbich

I honestly believe that a sense of humor is as vital to joy-filled memories as a pacifier is to a screaming baby's mouth.

For instance, when the apostle Peter said, "But do not forget this one thing, dear friends: With the Lord a day is like a thousand years, and a thousand years are like a day" (2 Pet. 3:8), he was explaining that the Lord is not slow; God's time is not our time. I suspect, however, that among his readers during those days there was at least one parent of a defiant teenager, grounded adolescent or baby with diarrhea who snickered out loud, then hollered, "Amen! You can say that again, Buster! One day is definitely like a thousand years!"

I had one of those "days" when [my son] Brian was about two-and-one-half years old.

Brian was in need of new shoes, and he hated anything new, including the mere suggestion.

"Guess what, Brian?" I say, as chipper as humanly possible.

"What!" he declares more than answers as he sits spellbound in front of the television while Bert and Ernie do their thing.

"Today's the day you get to pick out a brand new pair of shoes!"

"No. I don't want to."

"But Brian, you are getting to be such a big boy now. Your feet have grown so much your toes are touching the ends of your shoes."

"So?"

"So, we certainly don't want your toes to get crooked and start hurting."

"I don't care if they do."

"Well, I bet you're tired of looking at those worn-out old shoes? I know I am."

He takes the end of blankie that isn't trailing from his mouth and covers his shoes with it. "I don't look at them." He also doesn't look at me during any of this conversation.

"How about this? How about we get you a pair of gym shoes?" A daring suggestion since white, square-toed, leather high-top jobbies were about all anyone's child wore back then.

"No. NO NEW SHOES."

"But new gym shoes can run fast and jump high!"

"I CAN run fast. I don't want to jump high."

"You need them, Brian," I say through tightening lips.

"I don't want to go," he replies, just as tight.

"We have to go, Honey." I have read somewhere that using

terms of endearment softens the listener—and the message. "It's not a matter of whether you want to go or not, Sweetheart. This is not a discussion. You have to go."

In my wildest dreams I could not have foreseen what was to transpire.

We park the car and he reluctantly dawdles his way into the shoe store. We browse around at the rather large display of children's shoes. No matter which one I suggest, he hates it. He hates them all. He doesn't want white. He doesn't like colors.

> I have read somewhere that using terms of endearment softens the listener—and the message.

"They're dumb. They don't have any I like. Let's go home," he says. "I like my old ones."

I run through a battery of options:

(1) I can try to cram his foot into a shoe. I immediately rule this out because I don't have money to throw away on shoes that don't actually fit, and there will be no way to know for sure without a good measure on cooperative toes.

(2) I can whisk him back to the car. No dice. He will have won: his "NO NEW SHOES!" announcement will have prevailed.

(3) I can spank him, causing submission. Nasty scene in a shoe store. Brian's reaction to a spanking is not usually one of submission. Isolation works best for him, but then we're back to #2 which I have already ruled out.

(4) I can admit I don't know what to do. Right.

But I do know that love is patient, and patience is a fruit of the Spirit.

I go with #4 because I truly don't know what else to do, and I hope that through patience I'll learn what to do. Exhausted sigh follows this decision.

Firmly I grip his sweet little arm and lift him into one of the chairs. Nose to nose I explain that it is time to get shoes.

He counters my oh-so-firm announcement by sitting on his feet.

This is *not* the point in the story where I see how humorous the situation is. Many things flash through my mind; laughter is not one of them. I grab two shoes off the display area, blow a hair off my forehead and settle in.

"Can I help you?" a salesman asks, looking directly at Brian.

"No."

"Yes," I quickly counter. "Brian needs new shoes."

"Okay, big guy, let's have a measure, here." The salesman reaches beneath the chair next to Brian and produces the familiar silver appliance. Brian stares at him and doesn't move. I try to remain calm.

"Okay, son, let's see that growing foot." The man touches Brian's knee. Brian breaks eye contact and doesn't respond.

"Why don't you give us a minute?" I say. "We seem to need a little adjusting time."

"Fine. Just give a holler when you're ready." He retreats to behind the counter where the cash register is and I see him talking to the female cashier. She laughs. I do not.

Brian and I continue to sit in silence for what seems like an eternity. This could take longer than I planned on, but it will finally happen, I reassure myself. In the meantime, I just need to have patience…patience…patience…patience to come up with a plan.

While I'm busy entertaining the idea of hanging myself with a

24-inch shoelace from the display next to me (a plan I rule out as soon as I realize Brian still won't get any shoes), the salespeople smile at me as they pass by with armloads of boxes. Shoes other people and their children are buying. Some of them are getting more than one pair. Parents and their little darlings are chatting and laughing.

I am reminded of all the times laughter rings throughout our house. So much of it begins with Brian, too: his expressions, his natural bent to explore and the joy that comes with discovery, antics that delight and entertain, sweet and precious moments he gives us with kisses, hugs, and uncommon stories....

Minutes tick by. Brian's shins grow roots in the chair. Inner dialoguing runs rampant. Once a parent takes a stand, I silently tell myself, and after they have considered the rationale of the situation, if the original stand is correct, they should stick to it. That is the case here.

Waiting has become my plan.

Brian looks at me out of the corner of his eye and I swear he reads my mind. A couple more shovels of imaginary dirt can be seen flying over each of our shoulders as we dig our trenches a little deeper.

Brian has shifted several times but continues to harbor his feet under his buttocks. I'm sure his legs have fallen asleep and must be driving him nuts.

Suddenly, as he is mid-shift, I am swept with an overview of this ludicrous scene. My mind replays the laughably absurd day in its entirety and a laugh begins to rankle around in my throat. I make several attempts to swallow it down, but it bubbles and perks ever higher, until finally it erupts, startling the near-dozing Brian.

"What's so funny?" he asks.

"Oh, nothing. I was just thinking how silly it would be, sleeping here tonight. And if you'll excuse me, I need to make a couple phone calls. I've got to call Mrs. Gingell so she can let Bret know why no one will be home when he gets off the school bus. And I have to call Dad and tell him to go ahead and eat dinner on his way home, and not to expect us."

Brian's eyes nearly pop out of his head. I realize I'm on to something here. And so for good measure I added, "I'll tell Dad to bring us the sleeping bags and a flashlight. Bet it gets dark in here."

Brian says nothing. I, his mother, who has finally seen the humor in this war, sit next to him chuckling like a looney-tune. I thrash through my purse collecting change for the phone. "I'll be right back. Sit tight." I nearly lose control as this line slips out of my mouth. Like he needs a directive to do *that?* I'm hysterical. What a gas! "Sit tight," I repeat through waves of laughter. "Isn't that funny?"

Suddenly, one of Brian's legs slips out from under him. He cringes at the pain that comes from straightening out a locked joint. Then the other leg slowly unfolds.

"Okay," he says through a pout. "I'll get the dumb shoes."

Yes, the shoe-store memory is a good one all right, and we've shared it many times. I think back to it now whenever I walk into a shoe store. I'm just thankful I didn't have to find out what it's like to sleep in one.

Laughing Matters
Barbara Schiller

It was a great idea: A mother/daughter camping trip in the mountains with my 16-year-old, Serena. I had high hopes. We'd talk by firelight late into the night, we'd walk through the stillness of the woods, we'd bond and come home closer than ever.

The reality was a different story. Despite the bright blue sky, the fresh mountain air, the melodic song of the bluebird, Serena and I were at each other's throats. And we didn't even have our tent up yet.

As we hiked to our campsite, it was clear that Serena didn't want to be with me. She disagreed with me about everything and blamed me for imagined problems. I tried to make meaningful observations about the wonder of creation and the beauty around us, but she wasn't interested. Eventually, we settled into an uncomfortable silence.

When we reached our campsite, we argued about where to place the tent. We argued about what to have for dinner. We argued about which trails to hike the following day. Around 10:00 P.M. our volatile conversation escalated and we ended our first day of "bonding" with me in my sleeping bag on one side of the tent and Serena in her sleeping bag scrunched against the opposite wall, as far away from me as possible.

Suddenly, from the far corner of the tent, I heard laughter. Puzzled, I whispered, "Serena, what's so funny? The day has been so difficult." Her answer, quite frankly, shocked me.

"Mom, I think you take life way too seriously. Sometimes I love pushing your buttons, and then watching you react. You lose it over the littlest things. You get so intense sometimes!" And then she added tenderly, "Mom, don't you realize how much I'm like you? I need to lighten up. My friends tell me I'm intense, too."

Her words stung a little, but slowly, I began to laugh and laugh loudly. In fact, I laughed so hard tears were streaming down my face. Soon we were both laughing hysterically, unable to stop. The tension between us literally disappeared.

I crawled out of my sleeping bag and climbed over to Serena. In the darkness, I reached out my arms and we held each

"Mom, I think you take life way too seriously."

other. Laughter had penetrated both of our souls and we were altered. Silence returned, but this time it was different. This silence was the peace that is beyond our understanding. This contented moment was of God.

As I fell asleep, I realized it had been too long since I laughed like that, especially with my kids. The laughter had done more

than help Serena and me reconnect. It had provided a safe way for her to tell me something that was on her heart. It allowed me to hear something that I never would have heard had she confronted me in anger. Laughter had brought us together in a way my efforts to be deep and reflective had failed to do.

The next morning the sky was still bright blue and the mountain air still sweet. Nothing around us had changed. But we had. A quiet, unspoken serenity enveloped our campsite. We realized we had been given a precious gift, something we didn't want to leave behind in the mountains. We wanted to be like Moses coming down from Mount Sinai, glowing from his experience. Most of all, I didn't want to forget my daughter's words, or the lesson God had taught me about lightening my sometimes overloaded heart.

Proverbs 17:22 says it best, "A cheerful heart is good medicine, but a crushed spirit dries up the bones." Whatever is weighing heavy on your heart today, don't let it dry your bones. Let laughter refresh you. It is a medicine that truly creates growth.

St. Mom

Just about the time a woman thinks her work is done, she becomes a grandmother.

—BOB PHILLIPS

HI GRANDMA!!

Name It, Tame It

Karen Scalf Linamen

My six-year-old has a funny history with names. When she was first learning to talk, Kacie easily mastered words like "dog" and "apple" and "tea" (she's our native Texan, after all).

The word that she refused to say was "Daddy."

But it's not like she didn't have a name for him. She did. She called him "Mom."

Every night when she heard his key in the front door, she would drop whatever she was doing and race through the house, her arms outstretched in anticipation of a hug, her face glowing, all the while happily calling his name: "Mom! Mom!"

We tried everything we could think of to help her broaden her vocabulary, to no avail. Driving in the car, we would coach her. "Look, Kacie, this is DAD. Can you say DAD?" Sitting at the dinner table, we would quiz her. "Kacie, where's Mama?

That's right! Now where's your sister? Good job! Now where is Daddy? Kacie? Can you point to Daddy? Which one is Daddy? Hello? Kacie? Are you listening?"

Every time she called him "Mom," Larry gently corrected her and even threw in a bribe now and then. "I'm not Mom, I'm Dad. Can you say Dad? Please? Just say Dad. Say Dad and I'll buy you a new Fisher-Price tricycle. A new dolly. Season tickets for the Cowboys. A candy-apple-red Porsche. Anything!"

Then one night, everything changed. The battle finally came to an end.

Larry was sitting cross-legged on the floor in our bedroom, his tool box at hand, assembling a Sit-Up Master. (You've proba-

Can you say Dad? Please? Just say Dad. Say Dad and I'll buy you a new Fisher-Price tricycle.

bly seen the advertisements: "Flat Abs in Seven Minutes a Day! You'll Never Even Break into a Sweat! No Pain, All Gain! Look Like Cindy Crawford by Christmas! Buy Me! Buy Me Now!")

Yet I digress.

Larry was sitting cross-legged on the floor, sorting through nuts and bolts and pieces of pipe, when Kacie toddled over and plopped into his lap. She stayed there awhile, "helping" him with his task, while I lounged lazily on my stomach at the foot of our bed and watched the progress.

I hadn't moved a muscle in ten minutes when Larry, reaching for a tool, said nonchalantly, "Look, Kacie; Mom's working hard."

He's making fun of me! I thought, and I opened my mouth to object. But I never got the words out, because at that moment

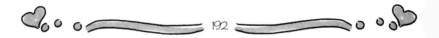

Larry went on to wave the Phillips in his hand and said, "See? This is a screwdriver, Kacie. Mom's using a screwdriver."

Suddenly I began to laugh.

Our battle was finally over. It ended the night Larry conceded, the night he threw in the towel and decided that a dad by any other name is still a dad.

Even if that name is "Mom."

The Future Is Coming
Lynn Assimacopoulos

The following is a school essay written by one of our sons, when he was 13 years old:

Ten years from now I will be at the University majoring in medical science. I'll be graduating and planning to be a great medical researcher. When I graduate I will go home first and visit my parents. Then I'll go to work at the University Hospital. After I have solved a number of questions about various common and some uncommon diseases, I will take a long vacation and set up my own laboratory in my basement of the medium-sized house I will buy. I might even start my own private medical practice. I will try to find cures to diseases such as cancer, heart disease and even the common cold. Hopefully, I will be successful and have a very smart assistant.

I also hope that I will have written many books and articles about the science of medicine. With the $100,000 I will make, I will buy a fancy car with an exterior of white wall tires, tinted glass, chrome plated accessories and a fine engine. The car will have an interior of velvet covered front and back seats, a real leather dashboard, an AM-FM stereo tape player, speakers in front and back, a built-in bar and television set, and of course, a telephone. And last, but not least, a shofer (he needed to learn to spell better). One of the trips I would like to make will be for my research; a trip to Africa to investigate the disease called sleeping sickness which is caused by the tse tse bug. The other pleasure trips I would like to make are to Paris, because I think it would be exciting to see the Eiffel tower for the first time, and I would also like to go to Greece and see where my father grew up. After that I would just take life as it is.

Now, let me suppose what I would have written when I was 13 years old:

Ten years from now I probably will not go to college but will become the secretary to the President of the United States, who will always be a Democrat of course. I will never go into the health field because sick people make me sick. (I went into Nursing.) I will get married to someone with a less complicated Norwegian last name than mine. Someone with a short, simple last name. (My married name is 14 letters long and Greek.) I will be a housewife as well as a very popular singer and dancer on the side. I will make several musical movies with famous singers and dancers and make a fortune from these and live in Hollywood, where I will actually own a

TV set and be able to afford to buy Tupperware. In my spare time I will write great poetry that will be read throughout the entire world. I will have 6 children (3 boys and 3 girls) and they will be perfect and never talk back to me and agree with everything I say because I will be the perfect parent. I will get a great amount of exercise every day and will be thin all my life. I will vacation in the jungles of Africa where there is no winter and no snow. After that I will take life as it is.

Taking life as it is. That's the hard part. Because it is never how we happen to see life at age 13.

After all that 13-year-old dreaming of being a medical scientist, our son is a band teacher. And a good one and that's where he belongs. He knew that when he learned to play his first instrument, a saxophone. He knew that when he received the Louis Armstrong Award in high school. He knew that when he developed a passion for jazz. He knew that when he enrolled in a School of Music at a university.

Instead of great poetry, I am writing nursing material about bedpans and stomach tubes.

His life is far from medical discoveries, far from $100,000 and far from fancy cars with chauffeurs. However, he has musical discoveries, a steady income and a Ford. And he does take life as it is and he is happy. That is what's really important.

I, on the other hand, never got to be a secretary to the President (I had to take typing twice), I am not thin, my last name is not simple and I cannot sing. Instead of great poetry, I am writing nursing material about bedpans and stomach tubes. I have not been the perfect parent and neither are my children perfect, but

all of us have tried our best to do the right things. My children still call, speak to me and like to come home once in a while.

We have three televisions and I have an entire drawer over-flowing with Tupperware. What more could a woman ask for? I have never been in the jungles of Africa and I live in the winter of the Midwest. More than half of my life has been spent at the bed-side of sick people. They do not make me sick. I am grateful that I could have some small part in their healing and in some cases in their passing from this earth. I was not meant to become a secre-tary, or a singer and dancer or go live in the jungles of Africa. I know I am where I should be.

I think all that God asks us to do is to accept where we are at this moment, on this day, at this time and at this place. And accept what we are and what others are. After all, He accepts us as we are whether or not we are making wonderful scientific discov-eries or becoming famous and whether we see ourselves as suc-cessful or not.

A priest once gave a wonderful sermon on what success really is. He asked, "Is it money? Is it fame? Is it expensive cars or other material things? Is it a very important high class job? Is it all kinds of good deeds?" His answer was very simple. "To God suc-cess is faith and faith alone. That is all we need and it is all that God expects from us." After that, as our son stated so simply, we can "take life as it is."

Skeletons in the Family Closet

G. Ron Darbee

Pssst...Psst...

The sound caught my attention as I slumped through the front door one evening, dragging my briefcase and eight of ten knuckles, my usual Monday night routine.

Pssst...Pssssst...Psssssssst!

There it was again, an annoying sound like a pest flying around your ear, urgently circling, looking for the opportune moment to attack. I brushed the phantom invader aside and set my briefcase down in its customary spot against the wall.

Pssssssssssstttttt!

"For crying out loud, what is that?" I said, slightly annoyed and accelerating toward full-scale aggravation. I shot quick glances from side to side, scanning the area for the offending source but catching sight of nothing.

"Shhhhh! They'll hear you!" A desperate whisper replaced the bug sounds and the familiar nose of my wife appeared as the closet door cracked open. "Quick, get in here."

"What are you doing in there?" I asked, more than a little puzzled with the sudden need for secrecy. "We're getting a little old for hide and seek, don't you think?"

She was in no mood for a game of fifty questions. With a firm grasp on my shirt and a half-dozen underlying chest hairs, she pulled me toward her into the closet. Her left hand reached for the knob and quickly, but quietly, drew the door shut behind us.

"Hi, Honey. I'm home," I said, not sure of the greeting etiquette demanded in these situations. "How was your day?"

"Hectic," Sue answered. "How about yours?"

"Typical Monday," I said, "but something tells me it went better than yours."

"Why don't we call it a tie and agree not to discuss it?" she suggested.

"Well now, I'd really like to go along with you on this one, Sue, but…it's just that we're having this conversation in a closet, and I'd feel remiss if I didn't ask for an explanation."

"Do you want the long or the short version?"

"Let's start with the short version," I said, "and you can fill me in on the particulars as necessary."

"All right," she said. "Dog, kids, telephone, doorbell." She delivered the sentence staccato, each word emphasized for maximum effect. Unfortunately, the lack of verbs and adjectives made her story sound more like a two-year old's newfound vocabulary than an explanation of her day's events.

"I'd like to buy a vowel, Vanna," I said. "I am completely unprepared to guess the puzzle."

She filled in the blanks: "The dog made a mess on the carpet, the kids have been arguing all day, the telephone hasn't quit ringing, and the doorbell stopped working sometime after the paper boy came to collect and before the mailman left this note saying he's sorry we weren't home. By the way, you need to stop at the post office on your way home tomorrow and pick up a package." She handed me a pink slip from the U.S. Postal Service.

"I hate to pry," I said, "but that still doesn't explain what you're doing in the coat closet."

"I needed some peace and quiet," she said.

"Honey, if this is how you get your peace and quiet, you're destined for a guest spot on *Oprah*," I said. "Wouldn't it be more comfortable if you lie down in the bedroom and shut the door?"

"They'd find me. They're smart, you know."

"Smart enough to chase you into the closet, anyhow," I said. "You know, Honey, you'll have to come out sometime."

"I have every intention on coming out—sometime," she said. "But for now, I have my flashlight, a good novel, and a place to sit down." She gestured toward an old milk crate we used to store files. "Let me finish my book in peace and quiet, and I'll be right out."

"What are you reading?" I asked.

"Tolstoy," she answered. "*War and Peace*. I promised myself I'd get around to it someday."

"I'll make you a deal, Sue," I said. "If you'll come out of the closet, so to speak, I'll handle dinner tonight and occupy the kids for a while."

"And answer the telephone?" she asked.

"And answer the telephone."

"It's a deal."

Sometimes I forget how hard it is being a mom. Not that I've ever been one, per se, but I have taken sole responsibility for the kids every so often. A couple of times, when Sue went on women's retreats, I was left to fend for myself. Admittedly, I never let our children chase me into a closet, but the thought of locking them in one (or two adjoining) certainly entered my mind.

Most of us dad-type fellows have it pretty easy when you get right down to it. We get up in the morning, kiss everyone good-bye, and enter a completely different world. We enjoy the inter-action of other adults, compete in the Afternoon Grand Prix on the way home, and return to find a family in reasonable order. Our kids don't take us for granted, because we're not there every minute of the day. Everyone's glad to see us, and life is good.

> Full-time moms remain on-call twenty-four hours a day and almost never get a vacation.

Full-time moms never leave the work-place. They remain on-call twenty-four hours a day and almost never get a vaca-tion. And home-school moms—now there's some gutsy women—they get the added benefits of attempting to impart an education between preparing meals and cleaning house.

That's a tough one for me to grasp, the idea of living where I work. I get jumpy when I spend an extra hour in the zoo I call an office; an entire night might send me over the edge. It was that thought that helped me find an answer to Sue's problem.

"Hey, Sue," I said, back in the hallway now and free of the smell of mothballs. "Why don't I take a long break tomorrow,

and we can meet for lunch. You pick the place. I'll call Kathy and see if she'll watch the kids."

"That would be nice," Sue said. "Maybe the years of hard work are beginning to pay off; you're turning into a thoughtful husband."

"Not thoughtful, Honey. Just frugal. I don't think our medical coverage extends to psychological. And, besides, I've got to eat anyway."

"Speaking of eating," Sue said, "what do you plan on making for dinner?"

"Who said anything about making dinner?" I asked.

"You did. You said you would make dinner, remember?"

"No," I reminded her, "I said I'd *handle* dinner. There's a difference."

"So how do you plan on handling it then?"

"Take-out, of course," I said. "I'll go and pick it up, and I'll even take the kids with me."

"Thank you for being so sweet," Sue said.

"No problem," I said, then playfully added, "but hey, rather than lounging around while I'm gone, see if you can figure out what's wrong with the doorbell." I exited quickly, before she sent *War and Peace* hurtling in my direction and waited for the kids in the car.

"Hey, Dad," Melissa said, climbing into the passenger's seat, "we had a really long game of hide and seek with Mom this afternoon. We never did find her."

"Oh, really?"

"No," she said. "Will you tell us where she was hiding?"

"Not on your life, Kid. Not on your life. But I have a better

idea," I said. "The next time you guys play hide and seek, why don't you play a trick on Mommy? Tell her to go hide and then don't even look for her. Won't that be funny?"

"Yeah!" Melissa said.

It was the least I could do for Sue, sweet guy that I am.

Chapter 17

Holy Motherhood

A mother is a mother still, the holiest thing alive.
—SAMUEL TAYLOR COLERIDGE

CarMa

Denise Roy

I have been driving a minivan for eleven years. This fact makes me, according to the market researchers who study such things, "a dull mom driving a dull car."

Okay, maybe I do fit the profile: a middle-aged mom with kids, a mortgage, ten extra pounds, and no chance of getting smiles from guys in other cars. But I get a little defensive when I see Internet chat rooms with topics such as "Minivans—When You Might as Well Be Dead." Mothers who still imagine themselves wearing motorcycle boots and listening to Jimi Hendrix write in to poke fun at those of us driving these wimpy mommy-mobiles. One mom wrote that driving a minivan "is like going around with a gigantic diaper tied to my ankle." Moms like this will only drive huge SUVs with smoked windows so they can put

the kids in the back and pretend they're still single and sexy. They don't fool me.

But I don't want to start another Mommy Wars. No matter what vehicle we drive—minivan, Urban Assault Luxury Vehicle, 1983 Suburu—let's face it: we're all spending more time schlepping kids around than we ever thought we would.

I just happen to drive an old Dodge Caravan with peeling blue paint and 110,000 miles. It has a lot of endearing qualities: a sliding door that rattles until you try to open it, and then it refuses to budge; French fries that are permanently wedged into the rear seat cushions; a rolling can of Diet Pepsi that keeps impersonating a broken transmission. My van is also a great storage unit. For instance, at this moment it contains the following: a plastic eyeball from Burger King, three weeks of school artwork, soccer socks that have stiffened beyond any hope of restoration, Magic Markers without caps, smashed Goldfish crackers, a broken cell phone that my mother insists I carry in case I break down on the freeway, a Halloween pin (it's now April), a squirt gun key chain, a pair of broken sunglasses, a packet of McDonald's ketchup, a tube of SPF-48 sunscreen, eight leaves, five receipts, four broken pencils, three French hens, two turtledoves, and an expired coupon for a car wash.

I always imagined I'd spend my days meditating, writing, maybe even changing the world in my spare time.

But then I grew up to drive a car pool.

So here's a math problem for you. If the driver of minivan A travels an average of ten thousand miles per year at an average speed of, say, thirty-five miles per hour and does this for eleven years, how many years of therapy will this driver need?

I read one woman's description of her vehicle as her "prison

on wheels." Another mom speaks fondly of her $%#@ van; she refuses to drive it on weekends. I know how they feel. It can seem endless out there on the road. Sometimes I get the feeling I'm going in circles.

Actually, I *am* going in circles. My usual car-pool route has a seven-mile circumference. Round and round and round I go, picking up children here, dropping them off there. It reminds me of a dog I had as a kid. Her name was Honey Bunch, and she looked like a miniature deer, with doe-like eyes and light brown hair. She was also clinically nuts. Apparently she had been weaned too young, which resulted in a variety of neurotic behaviors. The one I most identify with was her habit of circling the perimeter of our backyard, hour after hour; as a result, her paws wore a deep rut in our lawn. There are days when I'm convinced that my tires have worn a rut in the road.

Round and round and round I go, picking up children here, dropping them off there.

(I should note that Honey Bunch did have a variation in her routine: as she ran her laps, whenever she got to the spot just below our dining room, she'd take a giant leap up to peek in the window. This was great fun when guests came over for dinner. They'd be eating and conversing, and then every other minute they'd spot a brown flash out of the corner of their eyes. They'd look over, but see nothing. We'd time how long it took before they mentioned it.)

Sometimes I think my kids see me primarily as a chauffeur and that they might not even notice if another driver came and took my place. This thought occurred to me one Saturday afternoon. There was a torrential downpour, and while I would've preferred staying home by the fire, I had to get a package in the

mail. So Paul drove me to the post office in the minivan, parked at the curb, and waited while I jumped out with the package. After mailing it, I fastened the hood of my jacket and braced myself for a run back to the van. I dashed down the steps, pulled open the van door, and bounced onto the seat. "Whew!" I exclaimed, shaking out my hair. "It's wet out there."

Imagine my surprise when I looked over and saw a man I did not know sitting in the driver's seat and staring at me. A puzzled seven-year-old boy stood behind his father, his mouth gaping as he peered around the headrest. I must have been a little in shock, because it took a while for it to sink in: I was in the wrong van.

"Uh…I'm sorry," I apologized. "I thought you were my husband and this was our van."

"That's okay," the man smiled. "I thought you were my wife. She's wearing a very similar jacket."

I smiled awkwardly and opened the door. "Sorry," I said again, getting out. I gave them a little wave after I closed the door. I saw our blue minivan parked a few feet away, and when I opened the correct door, Paul had a big smile on his face.

"What were you doing?" he asked. "I watched the whole thing in my rearview mirror. I thought I had lost you for good!" he teased.

This event sparked some disturbing questions: What if we chauffeur moms are interchangeable? What if we got behind the wheel of any old minivan, and nobody really noticed, or cared? As long as we drive the car pool and get everyone where they need to be on time, would there be any complaints? I DON'T KNOW!!! Do you?

After one too many laps around the car-pool track, I was craving a few days when I wouldn't have to drive anyone anywhere. A

friend mentioned a silent meditation retreat that was being offered at a nearby monastery, so I traded car keys with my husband and went.

When I arrived at the retreat, I was shown to my own little monastic cell. It had a single bed, a small chair, a sink, a mirror, and a small closet. It was perfect. For three days I was served breakfast, lunch, and dinner. I had hours to pray and write and read. And I had nowhere to be, nowhere to go, nowhere to drive.

On the last day, I was sitting in the chapel, grateful for the silence and yet beginning to miss my family. As I sat there, I noticed that I was surrounded by beautiful stained-glass windows. And then the thought crept in: *My minivan has really stained glass windows.* Uh-oh, my mind was drifting. I brought myself back to the present moment, back to being transported by the angels to heavenly realms. And then I had another thought: *In my minivan, I transport the angels to heaven-knows-where. Stop it,* I told myself. *Get a grip.* Suddenly an onslaught of comparisons burst into my head: *In the monastery, I meditate. In my minivan, I mediate. In the monastery, psalms are sung. In my minivan, palms are flung. Repetitive schedules are found in both the monastery and the minivan: 8:00 A.M. chapel, 8:00 A.M. car pool; 3:00 P.M. chapel, 3:00 P.M. par pool; 6:00 P.M. chapel, 6:00 P.M. car pool.* The analogies continued against my better judgment. *Order pervades the monastery; odor permeates the minivan. One is filled with monks, one with punks…* I was starting to lose it.

And then I had a revelation. My monastery is not a silent cell out in the wilderness. My monastery is a minivan. It is also a kitchen, a child's bedroom, an office. My monastery is in the heart of the world—in family life, with a child on my lap, in my partner's arms.

It was time to go home.

The next day, as I was driving the car pool, I noticed a bumper sticker that read: "I'd Rather Be Fishing."

Not me. The bumper sticker I'd pick for my minivan would read: "I'd Rather Be Here Now." With the French fries and the children and the rattling door. A minivan might not be as good as a monastery for finding peace and quiet, but it is precisely the place where I find the face of God.

It's the Heart That Counts

Karen Scalf Linamen

I've been out of town.

I spent Mother's Day weekend speaking at the Terre Haute First Assembly of God, enjoying myself and falling in love with the wonderful folks at that church. I returned home Monday morning, pulling into my driveway at 2:00 A.M.

Four hours later, I was awakened by Kacie calling my name from her bedroom. Thinking she was having a bad dream, I hurried to her side.

She was still half asleep—in fact, her eyes were still closed—as she heard my voice and blurted, "Have you been to the kitchen table yet?"

I said no.

She tumbled out of bed with excitement. "Your presents are there! Let's go!"

"Kacie, it's six in the morning! Can't we sleep a while longer?"

She flashed me a look of sheer horror. "No! Your Mother's Day presents are there! We have to go right now!"

And so we did.

That's how I ended up, at 6:15 Monday morning, ooohing and aaahhhing over refrigerator magnets, a potted ink pen with a flower glued to the top, a handmade card, a new curling iron, and an iridescent purple blow-dryer. Larry's gift to me was a Mr. Coffee Iced Tea Maker.

I loved every gift.

I told Kaitlyn the curling iron was a brilliant idea, since my travels have made sharing the same curling iron a challenge (I never mentioned the fact that I bought my own curling iron in Terre Haute this weekend).

I told Larry the iced tea maker was great (I didn't mention that this is the THIRD iced tea pot he's bought for me, and that the other two are on a shelf in the laundry room because, in order to make tea, these machines require a pitcher full of ice, and I don't have an ice maker).

I realized that the real gift was the enthusiasm of the givers.

It was my turn, then, to give a few gifts. While on my trip, I picked up some sand-art kits for the girls and some candy.

Kacie was particularly excited about the candy. She gripped it tightly in her hand and beamed. "I had this kind of candy once before!" she said happily. "But it was too much sugar and it made me throw up!" She paused then, her smile frozen on her face and one eyebrow raised, as the implication of her statement sank in: Maybe candy that resulted in getting intimate with a commode wasn't such a great gift after all!

Thinking back on the morning, I had to laugh. So many good intentions! But even the best intentions didn't keep us from missing the target by a few inches on several gifts.

Did that diminish the experience for me?

Nah, somehow it just made the morning more precious.

And I realized that the real gift—the one that really glimmered against the backdrop of beautifully wrapped curling irons and tea makers, refrigerator magnets and blow-dryers—was the enthusiasm of the givers.

The real gift was the fact that Kacie's first thought after our separation was not about what I could do for her, but about what she could give to me.

The real gift was hearing from Kaitlyn that the iridescent purple blow-dryer cost more than the noniridescent purple dryer, but that she had been glad to pay the difference because she wanted me to have the very best one.

The real gift was the sacrificial efforts of a dad who has severe allergic reactions to malls and who has been known to wrap presents in trash bags.

God must understand this principle better than anyone.

That's why he cherished quarters from widows more than big bucks from hypocrites.

Have you ever thought about giving something to God—a song solo during worship service, an hour a week teaching Sunday school, participation in a local outreach or ministry—and then didn't do it because you were afraid your efforts would be less than perfect? Because you figured someone else could do the job better? Because you were terrified of making a mistake?

Yeah, me too.

What a shame.

Because the truth is that our heavenly Father cherishes the quality of our passion over the quality of our performance. He values sincerity over perfection. And he loves the givers more than he loves the gifts.

I need to remind myself of this often. Maybe even daily. In fact, maybe I should write myself a note and tape it to my bathroom mirror. It could remind me that my Father loves my heartfelt gifts to him—not because my gifts are perfect, but because he loves me with a perfect love.

I could ponder this each morning as I brush my teeth and wash my face.

Not to mention as I curl my hair, a shiny new curling iron in each hand.

Invisible Friends

Denise Roy

A few years ago we added a new member to our family. She doesn't eat much, and even though she's extremely quiet, she teaches us a lot.

I was introduced to her one day while I was reading the morning paper. Julianna, then two and a half years old, tugged at the sleeve of my robe.

"Mama, I have a new friend."

"Oh, really?" I asked. "Where is this friend?"

"Right *here*," she said, impatient at my inability to see beyond my nose.

"Oh. Of course," I wasn't sure what to ask next. "Is it a boy or a girl?" I ventured.

"A girl!" Julianna retorted.

"What's her name?" I asked.

Julianna tipped her head as if listening for the answer. Then she replied, "It's Abba."

I raised my eyebrows in surprise. I had never used this word around her. As you may know, in some languages, like Aramaic, it is the word for daddy or papa. It is also a name that Jesus used in addressing God.

I was so impressed by Julianna's obvious connection with the spiritual realm that I called to tell a friend the name of my daughter's invisible companion.

"Is that so?" my friend said upon hearing this. "Well, when my son was three, he had an invisible friend too."

"Oh, *really?* Well, what was *his* friend's name?" I asked.

"Poopy."

One day, Julianna was outside of church, balancing on top of a brick planter that was more than two feet high. I hurried over, afraid that she'd fall. "Honey, be careful," I said.

"When you feel the beat—that's where love is."

"It's okay. Abba is holding my hand."

She smiled and continued walking with absolute confidence.

It was a wonderful picture of what it looks like to trust in grace.

As I was putting Julianna to bed recently, she asked me to leave her room so that she could pray in private. I was surprised at her request; I left the room, but I couldn't resist peeking around the door to see what was happening. I saw her kneeling on her bed, her eyes closed, her hands folded in a perfect prayer position, facing a battery-powered lantern that was glowing on her headboard

(She and her dad had taken the lantern out the week before when they had camped in the backyard). She looked angelic.

After she was finished, Julianna yelled out that it was okay for me to come back in. I asked her where she had learned to pray that way.

"Abba taught me," she said quietly. I believed her.

One day, as we were driving to Toys "R" Us, Julianna called to me from the backseat.

"Mama?"

"What, sweetie?"

"I know where love is."

"Really? Where?" I asked.

"It's in your heart. Try this. Hold your breath, and put your hand on your chest. Do you feel it beating?"

I did as instructed. "Yes, I feel it."

"Love is right where the beat is. When you feel the beat—that's where love is."

Somewhat amazed, I asked, "How do you know this?"

"Abba told me. She crawled into my crib when we were both babies and told me that love is in the beat of your heart."

It's difficult to focus on driving when such messages are coming from the backseat.

Lest you think Abba is a complete innocent, let me set the record straight. Abba has made her share of messes around here, including scribbling on a wall or two. She doesn't always play games fairly, which frustrates Julianna. And sometimes Abba gets angry and moves back to her other home, which is okay, since then we don't have to worry about sitting on her.

Abba is not the only invisible friend we have around here, but she is the primary one. Others have shown up over the years, but they have come and gone. We also have angels living in our house, but they only come out at night. Julianna says that they dance in her room, and when they do, sparkles fill the air. So it was no surprise to me when I heard a radio interview yesterday in which a well-known religious teacher suggested that if people find formal meditation difficult, they might simply go into their child's room at night and meditate on the angels that are dancing through the air.

Sadly, I suspect that one day soon, Julianna will say there's no such thing as invisible friends. Abba and the angels will disappear. But maybe, just maybe, we will continue to feel the gentlest of touches or the quietest of presences, and we will realize that we are not alone.

Chapter 18

Smiling Strength

Alexander the Great's mother: How many times do I have to tell you—you can't have everything you want in this world!

—BOB PHILLIPS

Classy Womanhood
Angela Elwell Hunt

The sitcom ended to canned applause, and I rolled off the couch, ready to do my usual garbage collection sweep through the living room as I headed toward the kitchen. Suddenly the sitcom mother's image filled the screen—she was slender and designer-dressed, and every hair lay obediently in place. I could almost smell her expensive designer perfume.

I sniffed my hands. Eau de Wet Dog, mingled with the scents of supper.

"She's too classy to be real," I said, glaring at the woman on the television screen.

My husband lifted his brows.

"I mean, have you ever thought about it?" I continued.

"There's not a mother alive who is that classy."

After all:

- Classy women never show their toes in public. Mothers go barefoot as often as they can. In the winter they wear socks, even when they step out to fetch the newspaper from the driveway.
- Classy women are always dressed up. Mothers don't comb their hair before lunch on Saturday, and they undo that waistband button the moment they come through the front door.
- Classy women never yell. Mothers screech like loons when their children are bleeding, playing football, or about to do something they aren't supposed to do.
- Classy women read newspapers and ten-pound tomes on the *New York Times* best-seller list. Mothers read comics first thing in the morning and Dear Abby at lunch. At bedtime, mothers read dog-eared books about how to discipline their children properly.
- Classy women do not eat leftovers from their children's plates or lick the spoon after mixing chocolate icing. Mothers do, and consequently gain two pounds per child per year for the rest of their lives.
- Classy women cook exotic entrees like lamb and goose. Mothers order truckloads of pizza, know that thin hamburgers are better than thick ones, and can whip up a bowl of spaghetti in a pinch.
- Classy women never lose their dignity. Mothers hang dignity in a closet and pull it out only for things like family photos and parent-teacher conferences.

- Classy women don't cry at the sight of newspaper pictures or in hospital emergency rooms. Mothers do.
- Classy women watch PBS specials on television while they sip tea. Mothers guard the television with a vigilant eye, and know which circuit breaker to flip if things ever get out of hand.
- Classy women spend their evenings in quiet conversation with friends. Mothers spend their evenings with fathers, who know that nothing sends a child off to sleep faster than the sound of parents laughing in the kitchen.
- Classy women don't know how to change diapers, make relief maps out of dryer lines, or untangle a child's tongue from orthodontia. Mothers know everything.

I don't suppose we mothers can help it. Un-classiness is simply an occupational hazard. I used to want to be a classy woman. I spent hours designing my hair, planning my wardrobe, and polishing my manners. I read all the books about dressing for success and speaking with confidence.

But then God sent two wonderful children into my life and my priorities shifted. It became more important to raise happy, healthy, respectful children who knew and loved the God who loaned them to me.

A few summers ago I served as a counselor at middle school camp. My daughter and I joined several middle school kids for a horseback ride. As I swung into the saddle I asked the guide, "What's the name of this horse?"

The trail guide grinned. "Classy."

What a horse! Surrounded by squealing kids, horseflies, and

the thick stickiness of a Florida summer, she shifted under my weight and looked back at me with a calm, forgiving eye. I leaned forward and patted her neck, then held my head high. I was as close to Classy as I ever wanted to be.

Mrs. Perfection Meets Ms. Im—: The Proverbs 31 Woman

Patsy Clairmont

Does the Proverbs 31 woman have a name? I vote for "Mrs. Gets on Your Nerves" or "Mrs. I Have No Friends Because I'm So Perfect." I know. I know. I shouldn't think like that, but she is so squeaky clean it makes me want to oil her. Surely her joints must be stiff by now from holding everything together over the centuries. This gal needs a trip to a spa, a masseuse, or at least the local Jiffy Lube.

P-31 sounds like the wishful conjugating of a mother who wanted only the best of a woman's qualities for her son. Bible scholars suggest that King Lemuel was Bathsheba's name for Solomon. You know, a nickname like Lambie Pie or Dumpling. But the name Lemuel had deeper meaning ("belonging to God"). King Lemuel tells us in Proverbs 31 what his mama told

him about the kind of cloth an excellent wife is cut from. It's a heavenly fabric such as none of us has ever donned.

To be kind, I have to admit verses 10 through 31 list a number of worthy goals and a set of excellent standards for women. I know I need examples. In fact, some years ago (23 to be exact), I pleaded with the Lord to bring a woman into my life who would be a mentor, an example to me. His answer at that time was "I'm not going to give you an example; I want you to become one."

Don't think that didn't set my disorganized, unstable heart to palpitating wildly. I was more than willing to observe another woman living out truth, but to rise to the call of doing it myself—well, that was a mop of a different color. Believe me, a mop was the least of what it would take to clean up my act. I'm grateful that along the way the Lord eventually did send women who were excellent examples for me to learn from. But He has also required me to continue to grow up.

In reality I already had examples in my life, but I hadn't seen them for what they were. Perhaps you do, too. For me, it took time, healing, maturing, and personal experience before I realized what an example my mom had been. That insight came to me after I had stumbled over my fair share of personal failures that tenderized my heart and made me more merciful regarding others' failures.

You see, my mom didn't do everything right, but once I forgave her for not being perfect, I realized she did far more right than wrong. I encourage women today that, if they have issues with their moms, they resolve them as quickly as possible so they can enjoy their mothers and appreciate them. Before we know it, time flits by and our mothers are no longer with us.

My mom might not have been perfect like Mrs. P-31, but she sure was handy with her hands. She could organize, customize, and economize. She could take a shack and transform it into a cottage. She could take a chicken and concoct a feast. And she could take a nickel and create a bankroll. I don't know how she did what she did with what she had, but perhaps growing up in a large family on a farm, living through the Depression, and marrying a milkman gave her opportunity to be creative, versatile, resourceful, and industrious. Just like you-know-who, "Mrs. Got It All Together P-31."

Occasionally, I meet women who appear to have it all together, but on closer inspection (the old white-glove test), seldom is that true. I can say across the board that the people I've met are just that—people. They sometimes waste time, break the bank, burn the bacon, spew anger, and lose their way.

But that's what is so wearing about Mrs. P-31; no weaknesses are noted. This I know: If she does exist, I don't want to live beside her. I beat myself up enough already, thank you. You see, some days I leave lipstick in my jacket pocket and then launder the jacket, glazing my washing machine and dryer in Mambo Mauve. Other days I mail our taxes without the check in the envelope. The government, which has no humor, frowns on this. And then I scorch supper beyond recognition. (Actually, we aren't always sure what it is *before* I burn it.) So I'm not yet a P-31, or even a B-52 because I can hardly get off the ground to get my day going.

I console myself that I've made progress, and, dear sisters, if I understand this journey correctly, measurable, loving progress is what it's all about. P-31, in all her perfection, is an ideal to strive

toward. We won't reach her heights, but we're bound to be better just for trying, as long as we don't become tied to the earth by legalistically attempting to be perfect.

Proverbs 31 highlights wonderful ways a woman can effectively and even eternally reach out to others. Six times in this famous passage, hands are mentioned, and many more times they are implied, suggesting the incredible influence of a woman's touch.

I find I must first reach up before I can effectively reach out. So take my hand and let's call on Him together. With His help, we can change our world even if we are less than perfect.

Clean Sweep

Patsy Clairmont

Feeling zonked, I decided to zone out when I boarded the plane bound for home. I found my row and secretly checked out my seat companion. She was a normal, fiftyish-looking woman. (I immediately liked her for being older than me.) I peeked at her so I wouldn't be obligated conversationally. I didn't want anything to disrupt my siesta in the sky.

Doesn't it just drive you bonkers when you have a hidden agenda and someone toddles into your space and trips up your plan?

This time my "toddler" was a flight attendant who came scooting down the aisle offering treats. My stomach won out over sleep, and I ended up chatting with my neighbor, Susan. Am I glad I did! This was no normal woman.

Susan told me an incredibly sad story with a surprise ending.

She said her beloved husband of 30 years decided he loved someone else and wanted a divorce. The feelings of crushing betrayal deepened when Susan found out his affair had been going on for years. He was also a clever businessman and had prepared himself for this decision so that he would come out the financial winner.

Susan was first numb and then paralyzed by her grief. Her husband used her shock to his advantage, swooping down fast and furious to get all he could. Much to Susan's dismay, she was notified by the court that she would have to turn over to her husband and his girlfriend her cherished home of 23 years, where they had raised their five children.

Reeling from grief upon grief, Susan moved into a tiny, furnished apartment. There she tried to figure out what had gone wrong. In the divorce settlement, she was awarded a small, failing business, and that was to be her source of income. To add not only to her dilemma but also to her pain, her ex-husband and his female friend opened a new, competing business just down the street.

Now, folks, I don't know about you, but that's where I would throw my hands up and spit.

Not Susan. She reached inside and pulled up her faith. She decided she couldn't allow others' choices to extinguish her joy or decree her future. She was determined not to be a victim but to be victorious and begin with a grateful heart. No, she wasn't grateful for her tremendous loss, but that God is a healer of fractured hearts.

One day while doing dishes, Susan turned on the small TV near her sink. As she changed channels, she came to a musical presentation and was caught up in the contagious melody. But now she had no dance partner.

Then she spotted her companion leaning against the cup-

board. He was the tall, silent type. She waltzed over and embraced the kitchen broom, then twirled about the room, laughing and singing. Around and around she spun, dizzy with delight. Suddenly she realized she was not alone.

Susan saw she had been joined by three of her married daughters, who were standing in the doorway, giggling at their mother's antics. (They checked on her regularly those days for fear her losses would be more than she could bear, driving her to an act of despair.)

As she stood holding her silent partner, Susan looked at her girls and said, "In the years to come, may this be the way you remember me…dancing."

Susan didn't want to leave a legacy of brokenness or despair. Instead, she chose to give a living heritage of courage, conviction, and, yes, celebration. Her circumstances were anything but normal, but then, neither was her response.

By the way, she was able to turn the little business around, buy a lovely home, and enjoy a full and active life. She chose not to stay in her sorrow or linger in her loss, but in the midst of devastation, to dance.

Contributors

Lynn Assimacopoulos has been a registered nurse for forty years. She has published articles in professional nursing journals as well as poetry in anthologies. Lynn is married and has three grown children and four grandchildren.

Marti Attoun is a weekly humor columnist for her hometown newspaper, the *Joplin* (Mo.) *Globe,* and has published hundreds of articles in regional and national publications, including *Reader's Digest, Redbook, Christian Science Monitor,* and *Family Circle.*

Charlene Ann Baumbich is an author, speaker, and humorist who invites readers to drop by www.dontmissyourlife.com to find out just how fascinating she really is! She lives in Glen Ellyn, Illinois, with her husband, George.

Dr. Richard W. Bimler is president of WheatRidge Ministries in Chicago and is the author of several titles, including *Let There Be Laughter,* coauthored with his son. *Robert D. Bimler* is a businessman who works in Indianapolis.

Martha Bolton is a former staff writer for Bob Hope, two-time Angel Award recipient, Emmy nominee, and the author of more than thirty books, including *Didn't My Skin Used to Fit?*

Phil Callaway is an award-winning columnist, popular speaker, and author of such titles as *Who Put the Skunk in the Trunk?* and *I Used to Have Answers, Now I Have Kids.* He and his wife, Ramona, live in Alberta, Canada, with their three children.

Patsy Clairmont, a featured speaker at Women of Faith conferences, is the author of numerous best-selling books, including *God Uses Cracked Pots, Normal Is Just a Setting on Your Dryer,* and *Sportin' a 'Tude.*

G. Ron Darbee is the author of *Wrestling for the Remote Control* and *The Lord Is My Shepherd and I'm About to Be Sheared!* His award-winning short stories have been published in a wide range of publications.

Susan Duke is a best-selling author, inspirational speaker, and singer. She coauthored several titles, including *Courage for the Chicken-Hearted* and *Heartlifters for Women,* as well as the God Things Come in Small Packages series. She speaks in conferences, seminars, and churches nationwide.

Chris Fabry, a popular writer, broadcaster, and speaker, lives near Chicago with his wife and seven children. The former host of Moody Broadcasting's "Open Line" program, he is now heard daily on "Love Worth Finding" with Adrian Rogers. His books include *At the Corner of Mundane and Grace* and *The H.I.M. Book.*

Becky Freeman is an in-demand speaker and the best-selling author of numerous titles including the best-selling *Worms in My Tea* (coauthored with her mother Ruthie Arnold), *Peanut Butter Kisses and Mud Pie Hugs,* and *Chocolate Chili Pepper Love.* She and her husband, Scott, live in Greenville, Texas, with their four children.

Mary Hollingsworth is the best-selling author of over sixty titles. She is a freelance editor and has served as a leader in music outreach ministry for nearly two decades.

Joey Earl Horstman is assistant professor of English at Bethel College in St. Paul, Minnesota, and author of the popular, award-winning column "Channel Too" in *The Other Side* magazine.

Angela Elwell Hunt is the author of nearly one hundred titles,

including children's fiction, adult fiction, and adult nonfiction, and is the winner of a Gold Medallion award for *The Tale of Three Trees.* She and her youth pastor husband, Gary, are the parents of two teenagers.

Nancy Kennedy is the author of numerous books of humor and inspiration, including *Prayers God Always Answers* and *When He Doesn't Believe.* Her articles have appeared in numerous publications, such as *Christian Parenting Today.* She and her husband, Barry, the parents of two daughters, live in Inverness, Florida.

Carol Kent is a popular speaker, writer, and president of Speak Up with Confidence, a communications training ministry. Her books include *Speak Up with Confidence* and *Detours, Tow Trucks, and Angels in Disguise.*

Karen Scalf Linamen is the author of numerous books, including *Just Hand Over the Chocolate and No One Will Get Hurt.* She is contributing editor for *Today's Christian Woman* magazine and the author of more than one hundred magazine articles. Karen also speaks frequently at churches, women's retreats, and writers' conferences.

Mark Lowry is a comedian, musician, storyteller, author, and creator of the top-selling *Mouth in Motion* and *Remotely Controlled* videos. He appears in 150 events annually including touring with Bill Gaither and the Gaither Vocal Band.

Gracie Malone is a conference and retreat speaker, freelance writer, and Bible study teacher. Her articles have been published in numerous publications, including *Discipleship Journal, Moody,* and *Christian Parenting Today.* She and her husband, Joe, have three sons and six grandchildren.

Marilyn Meberg, a popular Women of Faith conference speaker, is the author of numerous titles including the best-selling *I'd Rather Be Laughing* and *Choosing the Amusing.* She lives in Palm Desert, California.

Dave Meurer is the winner of numerous state and national writing awards and honors. His articles have appeared in such major publications as *Focus on the Family* and *HomeLife.* He and his family live in northern California.

Nancy Chapman Monroe is an inspirational speaker and author whose writings have appeared in a wide range of publications, including *Decision, Good News,* and *Sunday Digest* magazines. She and her pastor

husband, Wayne, live near Atlanta, Georgia. For more information, visit Nancy's Web site at www.applefaith.com.

Joey O'Connor is a popular conference speaker and has authored books for a wide range of audiences, including couples, parents, and young adults. He and his wife live in San Clemente, California, with their three children.

Lindsey O'Connor is a full-time wife and mother of four, writer, speaker, and broadcaster. She has worked as a guest and broadcaster on such radio programs as "Focus on the Family" and "Point of View."

Kathy Peel is the author of numerous titles, including *Do Plastic Surgeons Take Visa?* She is a sought-after speaker at conferences and conventions, the founder and president of Family Manager, Inc., and a staff member at *Family Circle* and *Sesame Street Parents* magazines. She and her husband, Bill, live in Nashville, and are the parents of three sons.

Denise Roy is a mother of four, a psychotherapist, and the author of *My Monastery Is a Minivan.* She is also the founder of FamilySpirit, an organization that offers workshops and resources designed to nurture family spirituality (www.familyspirit.com).

Fran Caffey Sandin is the author of *See You Later, Jeffrey,* and a contributor to *The Strength of a Woman.* Her articles have been published widely in such publications as *Moody, Virtue, Focus on the Family Physician,* and *HomeLife.* She and her husband, James, are the parents of three grown children.

Barbara Schiller, B.S., M.A., is the founder and director of Single Parent Family Resources (www.singleparentfamilyresources.com), author of *Just Me & The Kids: Building Healthy Single Parent Families,* and a columnist who writes for several national magazines.

Lynn Bowen Walker is a freelance writer whose work has appeared in numerous periodicals, including *Marriage Partnership, Christian Parenting Today, Moody, Glamour,* and *American Baby.* She and her husband, Mark, live in Los Gatos, California, and are the parents of two sons.

Source Notes

Chapter 1: The Toughest Job You'll Ever Adore

"I Am Mommy, Hear Me Roar" taken from *Mom on the Run* by Nancy Kennedy. Copyright © 1996. Used by permission.

"Motherhood's Unsolved Mysteries" taken from *Happily Ever After...and 21 Other Myths about Family Life* by Karen Scalf Linamen. Copyright © 1997. Used by permission, Fleming H. Revell, a division of Baker Book House Company.

"The Husband's Progress" reprinted from *The H.I.M. Book.* Copyright © 1997 by Chris Fabry. Used by permission of WaterBrook Press, Colorado Springs, CO. All rights reserved.

Chapter 2: Home Is Where the Humor Is

"Why Coupons Are Ruining My Life" taken from *Mama Said There'd Be Days Like This* by Charlene Ann Baumbich. Copyright © 1995. Used by permission.

"The Big Mean Cleaning Machine: My Transformation into a Domestic Artist," formerly titled "A Clutter Bug Conspires to Clean Up

Chapter 3: Merry Perils of Motherhood

Chapter 4: Of Moms and Words

Chapter 5: Furry Fun

"Really, I'm Thinking of You" taken from *I'd Rather Be Laughing,* Marilyn Meberg, copyright © 1998, W Publishing Group, Nashville, Tennessee. All rights reserved. Used by permission.

"Who Loves Ya, Baby?" taken from *The Funny Farm* by Karen Scalf Linamen. Copyright © 2001 by Fleming H. Revell, a division of Baker Book House Company. Used by permission.

Chapter 6: Caution: Mother on the Loose

"Stuck Where I Did Not Belong" taken from *I Thought There Was a Road There* by Lynn Assimacopoulos. Copyright © 2000. Used by permission.

"I Don't Care How Famous You Are, I'm STILL Your MOTHER" taken from *Coffee Cup Friendship and Cheesecake Fun.* Copyright © 2001 by Becky Freeman. Published by Harvest House Publishers, Eugene, Oregon 97402. Used by permission.

"How My Son Saved Easter," formerly titled "The Easter Centerpiece That Almost Wasn't," by Lynn Bowen Walker. This article first appeared in *Christian Parenting Today* magazine (March/April 2002), a publication of Christianity Today, Inc. Used by permission.

Chapter 7: The Joys of Parenthood

"Haircut Wars" adapted from *Don't Miss Your Kids* by Charlene Ann Baumbich. Copyright © 1991 by Charlene Ann Baumbich. Used by permission of InterVarsity Press, P.O. Box 1400, Downers Grove, IL 60515. www.ivpress.com

"Summer Commandments" reprinted by permission of Chalice Press from *Praise, Anxiety, & Other Symptoms of Grace,* Joey Earl Horstman, copyright © 2000.

"There's Still Room to Spare for My Son's Fashion Feats" by Marti Attoun. This article first appeared in the *Christian Science Monitor* magazine (November 9, 2000). Used by permission.

Chapter 8: Mothering Rule #29: Embarrass Your Kids

"Peculiar Purpose" adapted from *Lemonade Laughter & Laid-Back Joy.* Copyright © 2001 by Becky Freeman. Published by Harvest House Publishers, Eugene, Oregon 97402. Used by permission.

"Phone Etiquette Gets Ringing Disapproval" by Marti Attoun. This article first appeared in the *Christian Science Monitor* magazine (August 24, 2000). Used by permission.

"The Talk" taken from *Let There Be Laughter,* page 48, by Richard W. Bimler and Robert D. Bimler, © 1999 by Concordia Publishing House. Reprinted with permission.

Chapter 9: Mothering Rule #30: Get Embarrassed by Your Kids

"Who's Doing This?" taken from *Fireside Stories of Love and Laughter,* Mary Hollingsworth, copyright © 2000, W Publishing Group, Nashville, Tennessee. All rights reserved. Used by permission.

"Top 5 Ways to Spot a Mother on a Date" excerpt by Becky Freeman taken from *Courage for the Chicken Hearted.* Copyright © 1998 by Becky Freeman, Susan Duke, Rebecca Barlow Jordan, Gracie Malone, and Fran Caffey Sandin. Used by permission of RiverOak Publishing, Tulsa, OK. All rights reserved.

"Foxes in the Henhouse" excerpt by Fran Caffey Sandin taken from *Courage for the Chicken Hearted.* Copyright © 1998 by Becky Freeman, Susan Duke, Rebecca Barlow Jordan, Gracie Malone, and Fran Caffey Sandin. Used by permission of RiverOak Publishing, Tulsa, OK. All rights reserved.

Chapter 10: Life with Mr. Comedy (a.k.a. "Dad")

"Superdad's Holiday Adventure" taken from *I Used to Have Answers, Now I Have Kids.* Copyright © 2000 by Phil Callaway. Published by Harvest House Publishers, Eugene, Oregon 97402. Used by permission.

"You Rile the Kids Up, You Put 'Em to Bed!" taken from *Women Are Always Right and Men Are Never Wrong,* Joey O'Connor, copyright © 1998, W Publishing Group, Nashville, Tennessee. All rights reserved. Used by permission.

"Thar She Blows" taken from *Daze of Our Wives* by Dave Meurer. Copyright © 2000 Bethany House Publishers. Used by permission.

Chapter 11: Cooking Up Comedy

"A Baking Recipe for Mothers" taken from *Peanut Butter Kisses and*

Mudpie Hugs. Copyright © 2000 by Becky Freeman. Published by Harvest House Publishers, Eugene, Oregon 97402. Used by permission.

"A Smashing Success in the Kitchen" taken from *Sometimes I Wake Up Grumpy...And Sometimes I Let Him Sleep* by Karen Scalf Linamen. Copyright © 2001 Fleming H. Revell, a division of Baker Book House Company. Used by permission.

"My On-and-Off Struggle with Manuals" by Marti Attoun. This article first appeared in the *Christian Science Monitor* magazine (October 18, 2001). Used by permission.

Chapter 12: Family Frivolity

"In the Clutches of Summer" by Marti Attoun. This article first appeared in the *Christian Science Monitor* magazine (August 23, 1999). Used by permission.

"The Roosters in Our Family Tree" excerpt by Gracie Malone taken from *Eggstra Courage for the Chicken Hearted.* Copyright © 1999 by Becky Freeman, Susan Duke, Rebecca Barlow Jordan, Gracie Malone, Fran Caffey Sandin. Used by permission of RiverOak Publishing, Tulsa, OK. All rights reserved.

"Guest of Honor" taken from *If Mr. Clean Calls, Tell Him I'm Not In!* by Martha Bolton. Copyright © 2000. Fleming H. Revell, a division of Baker Book House Company. Used by permission.

Chapter 13: Those Amusing Adolescents

"A Mother's Instructions to Her Teenage Driver," formerly titled "Because I Love You," excerpted from *Dance with Me, Lord!* © 2001 by Nancy Chapman Monroe. Used by permission.

"A Mother's Guide to Cool" taken from *The Stomach Virus and Other Forms of Family Bonding,* Kathy Peel, copyright © 1993, W Publishing Group, Nashville, Tennessee. All rights reserved. Used by permission.

"When I Lost the Need to Know" taken from *I Thought There Was a Road There* by Lynn Assimacopoulos. Copyright © 2000. Used by permission.

Chapter 14: Kids Will Be Kids

"Let There Be Light" taken from *God Things Come in Small Packages*

for Moms by Susan Duke, et al, 2000, Starburst Publishers, Lancaster, PA 17601. www.starburstpublishers.com. Used by permission.

"Relatively Perfect" taken from *Out of Control* by Mark Lowry, copyright © 1996, W Publishing Group, Nashville, Tennessee. All rights reserved. Used by permission.

"Letter from Camp" taken from *Let There Be Laughter,* pages 55–57, by Richard W. Bimler and Robert D. Bimler, © 1999 by Concordia Publishing House. Reprinted with permission.

Chapter 15: Where There's Motherhood

"Laugh and Lollygag" taken from *If Mama Ain't Happy, Ain't Nobody Happy!* Copyright © 1996 by Lindsey O'Connor. Published by Harvest House Publishers, Eugene, Oregon 97402. Used by permission.

"When All Else Fails, Laugh" adapted from *Don't Miss Your Kids!* by Charlene Ann Baumbich. Copyright © 1991 by Charlene Ann Baumbich. Used by permission of InterVarsity Press, P.O. Box 1400, Downers Grove, IL 60515. Web site: http://www.ivpress.com.

"Laughing Matters" by Barbara Schiller. This article first appeared in *Christian Parenting Today* magazine (March/April 2001), a publication of Christianity Today, Inc. Used by permission.

Chapter 16: St. Mom

"Name It, Tame It" taken from *Sometimes I Wake Up Grumpy...and Sometimes I Let Him Sleep* by Karen Scalf Linamen. Copyright © 2001 by Fleming H. Revell, a division of Baker Book House Company. Used by permission.

"The Future Is Coming" taken from *I Thought There Was a Road There* by Lynn Assimacopoulos. Copyright © 2000. Used by permission.

"Skeletons in the Family Closet" taken from *Wrestling for Remote Control* by G. Ron Darbee. Copyright © 1996 by Broadman & Holman Publishers. Used by permission.

Chapter 17: Holy Motherhood

"CarMa," from *My Monastery Is a Minivan* by Denise Roy, published

"It's the Heart that Counts" taken from *The Funny Farm* by Karen Scalf Linamen. Copyright © 2001 by Fleming H. Revell, a division of Baker Book House Company. Used by permission.

"Invisible Friends," from *My Monastery Is a Minivan* by Denise Roy, published by Loyola Press in 2001, is reprinted by permission of Loyola Press. For more information or to order a copy of the book, call 1-800-621-1008.

Chapter 18: Smiling Strength

"Classy Womanhood" taken from *My Life as a Middle School Mom* by Angela Elwell Hunt © 2000 by Angela Elwell Hunt. Published by Servant Publications, P.O. Box 8617, Ann Arbor, Michigan 48107. Used with permission.

"Mrs. Perfection Meets Ms. Im—: The Proverbs 31 Woman" taken from *I Love Being a Woman* by Patsy Clairmont, a Focus on the Family book published by Tyndale House Publishers. Copyright © 1999 by Patsy Clairmont. All rights reserved. International copyright secured. Used by permission.

"Clean Sweep" taken from *Normal Is Just a Setting on Your Dryer* by Patsy Clairmont, a Focus on the Family book published by Tyndale House Publishers. Copyright © 1993 by Patsy Clairmont. All rights reserved. International copyright secured. Used by permission.